CW01313490

THE BEST LOSER

We are all losers at some point in our lives,
some of us are just better at it than others.

This autobiographical book is just one man's viewpoint
of what it means to be a loser.

By

Mark Mooney BEM

Copyright © Mark Mooney 2015

Mark Mooney has asserted his right under the Copyright, Design and Patents Act 1988 to be identified as the author of this work.

This book is a work of non-fiction based on life, experiences and recollections of the author. In some cases names of people, places and details of events have been changed and characters created for artistic purposes and to protect the privacy of others.

ISBN – 10: 1506019641 Mark Thomas Mooney
ISBN – 13: 978-1506019642

All photos are courtesy of the author except for those published on pages 115-116 which were kindly donated by © Michael Reed

The front and back cover were created by the author using licensed images purchased from Fotolia.com
#75823210 | Author: © Sergey Nivens

All rights reserved. No part of this book may be reproduced, stored in a retrieval system, or transmitted in any form or by any means, electronic, mechanical, photocopying, recording or otherwise, without the prior written permission of the author.

CONTENTS

Acknowledgements   v

Preface   (Please read its fundamental to the book)   viii

Chapter 1. The Best Loser   1

Chapter 2. New Beginnings   14

Chapter 3. Making a Million   22

Chapter 4. Making a BIG Mistake   28

Chapter 5. Unbelievable   36

Chapter 6. Bourne Identity   49

Chapter 7. Procrastination The Death of a Business   57

Chapter 8 More Dark Days Ahead   64

Chapter 9. Quit to Succeed   79

Chapter 10. From Pillar to Post   86

Chapter 11. Education, Education, Education   91

Chapter 12. On Reflection   96

Chapter 13 My Earliest Memories   99

Chapter 14. Fearless   104

Chapter 15. Moving House   121

Chapter 16. Big School, New Friends, Free Dinners   128

Chapter 17. Bikes and Bogies   135

Chapter 18. How Things Can Quickly Change   139

Chapter 19. Taking The Queens Shilling   144

Chapter 20. Leaving Home	149
Chapter 21. Passing Out	158
Chapter 22. The Bermuda Triangle	164
Chapter 23. 18 Years Old & Engaged to be Married	171
Chapter 24. Lizards a Jail Sentence and a Goat	175
Chapter 25. Quite Simply Dear John It's Over	182
Chapter 26. New Baby, New Car Plus Mountain of Debt	187
Chapter 27. Belfast 80-81	191
Chapter 28. Time in the Sun	197
Chapter 29. Not Ireland Again	206
Chapter 30. Back to Basics	219
Chapter 31. Promotion, Pneumonia and a Big Bang	229
Chapter 32. Helicopter, Dancing Girls & Medals	250
Chapter 33. Married Live V The Promotion Ladder	257
Chapter 34. Living Separate Lives	262
Chapter 35. The Final Push to Success	267
Chapter 36. Time to Hang up My Boots	272
Chapter 37. So Now What?	277
Chapter 38. Back to The Future	281
Chapter 39. Not Quite The Final Chapter	287
Epilogue	289

ACKNOWLEDGEMENTS

It doesn't matter what I write here because very few people read this part of a book anyway, some may give it a casual glance to see if they are listed, others will just thumb through to the first chapter missing it out completely. Nevertheless I also know that some of you will read every word I have to say. So in true tradition of personal acknowledgements, I would like to take this opportunity to mention a few people.

For years now I have wanted to write a book, I think it's something we all say at some point in our lives, or its something someone else will say to us. Especially after we recall a particular moment or hilarious episode in our lives, which we are eager to share with others. After which they utter those immortal words…

"Hey Mark, you should write a book".

Like many people I have lived most of my life putting things off until another day; this book is testament to that. I actually started writing this book almost five years ago. At the time I was fighting depression and feeling sorry for myself. When I first started writing I decided not to tell anyone as I wasn't sure if it would ever be published, or if I had done anything interesting enough to warrant getting it published. I doubted myself; I had lost my confidence, my self-esteem. Just a few months before I started writing I still had thoughts of ending my life; I was looking for a way out, I was in a bad place. Over the years I had read lots of self-help books looking for answers, it never actually dawned on me at the time of reading these books that the best self-help book is in fact the one you write yourself. Depression is quite possibly something we will all face at some point in our lives. I now know from experience that there are no drugs that can cure depression they only suppress the feelings, please note that no drugs or performance enhancing stimulants were taken during the publication of this book, (*sorry private a joke*).

In normal circumstances the acknowledgement section of a book is used to thank all the people who have helped to put this book together, or the people who have inspired me, supported me, and guided me. I could just say you know who you are, as there have been many over the years, so if your name is not mentioned here please don't be disappointed. If you know me personally then you can count yourself as a contributor to this book, as I like to think that I am influenced by everyone I come into contact with, in one way or another. So to you all, I say thank you; however there are some I would like to mention.

So in true tradition like a speech at an award ceremony, but without the tears, here is a list of people I would like to thank. One of the first people I must thank is actually a guy from work, I thought I made the mistake of telling a number of people that I was writing a book, undoubtedly I got a few blank looks. Although one did offer me words of encouragement, and ever since the day I told him he constantly badgered me every fecking time he saw me. At one point he even got me to set a deadline, which I never actually kept, obviously. But his constant reminders and nagging did get me to finally finish the book. So Nick you know who you are, thank you for the encouragement. I hope I can return the compliment when you finally sit down to write yours. I would also like to thank you for ticking all the right boxes when you interviewed me for the job, to be honest if I hadn't been successful that day who knows what would have happened, so thank you my friend.

Many of the people I would also like to thank are no longer with us, but without doubt they have shaped my life in one way or another. My mum, who I miss so much now, my stepdad Gerald, who played a vital part in looking after my younger brother and sister, my uncle Albert & aunty Norah, who treated me as the son they never had, thank you all for being you. I would like to thank my own siblings, my younger sister Sharon and youngest brother Paddy for all the support you have given me especially during my darker days. My big brother Mick for showing me that no matter what life throws at you, you just get on with it and soldier on. I couldn't finish this section without thanking the most important people in my life, my wife Linda who is always there when I need her, the girl I fell in love with at the age of fifteen, you don't give yourself enough credit for what you do. My three sons Mark, Thomas (Tom) and Louis, I hope this book helps to fill in the some of the gaps created by my absence during those earlier years.

Finally we are often asked, *"If you could pick just one person who has influenced you most in your life, who would that be?"* For me there is one simple answer… My Dad, and the person I dedicate this book to.

PREFACE

A young teenage boy was standing by the graveside of his father, showing no emotion, no feelings for this tragic loss; he did not weep or shed a single tear, he just stood there on that cold wet Monday morning in November. His freezing gloveless hands in his pockets, quietly looking down at the open grave, staring at the name engraved on the plaque on the coffin. A fine cold mist of rain covered his face, a feeling of emptiness surrounding him. Was he still in shock from the news he had received just 10 days ago? When on that normal Saturday morning this teenage kid quietly closed the front door at 6.30am as he left the house to do his paper round. Everyone else was in bed the house was quiet, cold and dark as usual. When he returned home just a few hours later, he noticed that there were cars on the street outside his house. Although it's common to see this today, back in 1974 it was not the norm, very few people owned a car back then.

Swinging open the tall green back gate he walked through the small yard to the back door, pushing and ducking his way through the low hanging washing, pegged out to dry in the cold mid-morning air. He opened the door to see faces of people he had never seen before, some he recognised as aunties and uncles, for a moment no one spoke a single word. It was that silence we all feel when we know something is wrong, it's as if time stops and you're the only person moving, breathing, all eyes fixed on you.

All he remembers from that day was the vision of his mum standing at the kitchen sink to his left, wearing that same floral pinney she always wore, washing pots as usual and probably making tea for all those guests. Suddenly the silence was broken, she turned around and said **"your dad's dead"**; no build up, no prior warning that something this tragic had happened in the early hours of that morning on Saturday 26th of October 1974.

Perhaps this was the best way a mother could tell her 14 year son, quickly and simply, to the point with no fluff, just the cold hard fact that he was dead. There was no how or why. Just the planting of a permanent memory, one that last's a lifetime.

This is his journey, my journey. A book any of us could write, if only to prove that we all have a story to tell, no matter how unimportant we think we are. A simple book that illustrates that we can do anything, if we choose to, the path we take in life is quite simply our choice. Many of us walk a similar path on life's journey, as we enter the maze of twists and turns, ups downs and disappointments. We are all losers at one point or another, lost and often misguided, until we find our way out. Unfortunately the way out is not always the same for everyone.

x

Chapter 1

The Best Loser

The bell sounded for the final round, both boxers walked to the centre of the ring touched gloves in acknowledgement of sportsmanship and respect they had for each other. They say that as we get older we all remember the time when we were twenty one, in our prime the world at our feet ... Let me start by taking you back to the time when I was in my prime, with a full head of hair, with shoulders, arms and six pack abs like a miniature Arnold Schwarzenegger, the only trouble was I seemed to have legs from another body. I looked like one of those kids flip books where you swap the top and bottom half of bodies. I put this down to the Army's obsession with deploying Multi Gyms to all the outposts in Northern Ireland. As this was the only recreational equipment we had during the 1980's. Those of you who may remember those blue metal monsters will know that the only two things that still functioned after continuous pounding, were the bench and shoulder press stations. Like many would-be bodybuilders, I'd spent that six months bench pressing my way through the tour, not to mention munching my way through a mountain of desiccated liver tablets and raw eggs. But more on that later.

My real story begins on cold October morning in 1981 while serving in the Army based in Minden in Germany. It was the day I was picked for the Inter Company Annual Novice Boxing Competition. I was going to use the word selected as this would imply that I was the best or at least the most suited for the job, based on a god given talent for boxing; however this was not the case, as I was simply picked based on my weight at that particular time, or was it simply the fact that I looked good in a vest?

The Boxing Competition was a fearlessly fought contest, and normally the culmination of the prestigious accolade of being the Champion Company. It was also the time when most of the company sergeant majors would have big money riding on this event, therefore getting all your boxers to the finals was paramount to this success.

The start of the competition was just four weeks away, our man was keen to win, he was old school. A thirty something CSM (Company Sergeant Major), named Mick Moran. In his words a fuckin hero, a recipient of the prestigious Queens Gallantry Medal, QGM, earning him the nickname "Metal Micky", due to the number of medals he wore on his chest. His main focus for motivation was that you were repeatedly told quite bluntly that *"First is First and Second is Fucking nowhere"* he was a real motivator, winning was the only outcome. In a strange way I admired him.

Getting picked for the team was based on a simple system, which quite possibly is still used in the armed forces today. We lined up in size order, tallest on the right short arses on the left. That word of command still echoes in my mind, "TALLEST ON THE RIGHT AND SHORTEST ON THE LEFT IN SINGLE RANK... SIZE"! We would all scuttle around for a few minutes finding our place in the line. I knew my place was down the end, with all the other short arses. One of the platoon sergeants would walk down the line and place a set of cheap NAAFI bathroom scales in front of you, and in true military fashion you took a pace forward stepped on the scales, and stood there while your weight was announced to the Sergeant Major...

"Mooney 10 stone 8lbs..." "Not another fucking Welterweight, we'll soon get you down to Light Welter Mooney lad". The reality was, you never got to box at your natural weight you always had to work off those extra pounds, apart from the biggest guy in the company, he was deemed the super heavyweight regardless if he could box or not. The other natural heavyweights these were the guys over 12 stone would be forced to box at light heavy, the light heavyweight would have to slim down to middleweight and so it went on. Making the weight for the bout was critical to the success of the team. Those four weeks of training were tough and losing the weight was hard for me, especially when you are already carrying a lot of muscle. The drying room became a second home for many of us. This was where we would shed those extra pounds. It was like a sauna but without the steam. Its real purpose was for drying wet kit, but during the boxing season it was the equivalent to the hole, the slammer, a crazy place where you would find grown men dressed in black bin liners and NBC suits skipping to the "Rocky theme or The eye of the Tiger" on constant loop. Not forgetting the additional reminder from the Sergeant Major that "first is first and second is fucking nowhere".

Then came the competition, after a few preliminary bouts beating my opponents, one by way of knockout and the others on points, I made it to the final and although it wasn't Madison Square Garden or the Wembley Arena this was a big event. It was always held in the evening with the officers and warrant officers in there finery, plus a few honoured guests from neighbouring Regiments within the garrison. Almost eight or nine hundred people crammed into the large gymnasium. All wanting to see two young men box the crap out of each other, no head guards no big daft sixteen ounce gloves this was Novice Boxing at its best. You would be surprised how much damage can be done in just three short rounds.

So the final came, it wasn't long before it was my time to box, I stepped into the ring to face this guy who I met briefly at the weigh in earlier that day, he was about 6ft seemed quite tall for a light welter weight… probably because his company sergeant major made the natural middle weight slim down to light welter, this guy was huge compared to my 5ft 6in frame. Not only that, after the morning weigh in he had spent all day in the NAAFI munching on pies and donuts, so he was now probably at his natural weight.

As the fight went on, it was punch for punch for three consecutive rounds, but in the second round he had caught me on the side of the nose, it wasn't that it was a big punch but enough to cause my nose to bleed and by the end of the second round blood was all over the place, the crowd loved it. It was the classic David and Goliath match, a little guy fighting a man, who was taller and in my opinion now much heavier than me. In the third round I was rocking his head back with every punch. At the end of the bout there were over 800 people all thinking the same as me. (*I'd won*).

We stood in the centre of the ring with the referee holding our wrists the master of ceremonies announced that the referee would like to congratulate both boxers on a well fought courageous contest. The crowd erupted with applause I could hear people chanting my name *Mooney, Mooney, Mooney*. Then came the announcement, the winner of the Heart's Medal Inter Company Light Welter Weight Class, there was a long pause it was like waiting for the announcement at one of those award ceremonies… is by a majority decision. I could feel the grip from the referee on my wrist tighten, majority that meant that I had won on points. I just knew he was going to raise my hand the grip got tighter… in the RED Corner… that voice inside my head said… hang on I'm in the BLUE Corner. I glanced over to check, then he announced the name, Fusilier BELL… who? Until that moment I don't even think I knew his name …. Ding, ding, it dawned on me I had been beaten by a Bell.

Most people are saved by the bell, not this loser. I felt that pain of defeat run through my body that voice inside my head saying "First is first and second is fucking nowhere. I looked up, I could feel the emotion vibrating in my soul, and although it was only three rounds of novice boxing I'd given my all, surely that counts for something.

I did everything my corner man asked me to do, but I stood there in defeat my head then sank as I walked quietly to my corner. I bowed to the officials and ducked under the second rope to take that long walk of defeat back to the changing rooms.

I was told a little later that on my scorecard one of the judges had marked me down by a single point, just one more punch would have done it, one simple double jab that's all it needed and the result would have been very different. I got two medals that night which I still have today; one says Light Welter Runner up. The other was awarded to me in the final presentation of the evening; this was the medal that went to the BEST LOSER.

This was normally given to a fighter who lost in a valiant effort in the preliminary bouts. It was the first time it was awarded to a finalist. I should have been proud, I smiled and took my bow once again to thunderous applause but inside I knew that I had just stood in front of over 800 people, branded as a loser not just a loser but the BEST LOSER. I could see it engraved on the medal. I was now officially one of life's losers, however at the time it became more of a positive than a negative. For a few days after guys who I never even met before, even the officers would come up to me and say *"great fight you should have won that one Mooney"*. I didn't know it at the time but what I failed to realise was that although I was in my mind one of life's losers, I was in fact remembered.

Being remembered is what counts and most of us know this. It's what you are remembered for that matters. Was I just the loser or the gutsy little guy who not only had the courage to step into the ring in the first place, something that many would not even dream of doing? Not only did I step into the ring I fought my heart out because I truly believed that *"First is First and second is fucking nowhere"*.

I had arrived in Germany in August 1979, was promoted to Lance Corporal shortly after, and by the summer of 1981 I was a young 21 year old Infantry Corporal. In September 1983 I was promoted to Sergeant, so in less than four years I had gone from the rank of Fusilier (*Private Soldier*), to Sergeant. Believe it or not, back then it was rare for a mainstream infantryman to be a Sergeant at just 23. I wasn't promoted for my skills as a boxer, I only boxed a few more times after the night I became the BEST LOSER, unlike one of my fellow team mates who later became the famous Dark Destroyer, and Middleweight World Champion, the infamous Fusilier, Mr Nigel Benn.

So what was it that propelled me forward, was it just the natural progression of being in an environment that thrived on promotion or was there something more. Was this loser simply driven by the power of losing? Was I just one of those guys who were in the right place at the right time? We often hear this from others, or on occasion say it ourselves when jealous of someone's achievement… *"Yeah it's alright for you, you were in the right place at the right time mate"*. What we forget is how we/they got to be in the right place; we forget that getting there can sometimes take a long time. But it's not as simple as just being in the right place and I am sure you know this too. It's also opportunities that matter. Sometimes they come your way and we fail to take them, it's like running for the bus, we make an effort see it passing us by, so we slow down and give up, sometimes pretending we weren't even running for it in the first place and say sod it, I'll wait for the next one... sometimes this is a long wait. That opportunity has gone.

Humour me while I expand on this metaphor... We can on occasions be standing at one of life's bus stops and the bus goes past, we think we are in the right place, perhaps we are standing at the wrong stop for that particular bus, or we simply failed to put out our hand to indicate to the driver that we want to get on... as we watch it sail past, an opportunity missed because we failed to notify the driver that we wanted to get on. Not only do we have to be in the right place, have the opportunity, most of all we need to take action and get on.

Before I was promoted to Sergeant I was offered the opportunity to host the Annual Christmas Review. This was yet another big event in the military calendar. The whole Battalion over 650 soldiers, plus wives girlfriends' kids etc. would all be attending this event, a similar size crowd to the boxing finals and also staged in the gymnasium, as this was the biggest venue on the camp.

The Christmas review was a well organised show put on to entertain the masses, it was something that was often done to raise moral, an opportunity to get everyone together, quite often prior to a major deployment/ operational tour. On this particular occasion it was another two year stint in Northern Ireland. I suppose if it was done today it would be called something cheesy like *"The Battalions Got Talent"*. I can bet someone has actually done that.

The Best Loser

Each company would produce an act most of which comprised of a skit or involving some kind of humours attempt to have a stab at the system, mainly in-house humour, based on past events or personalities. It was also a time for the guys who did have a natural talent i.e. to sing, play a guitar, do some magic, a bit of stand up etc, basically a rare opportunity to perform on stage in front of a bigger audience. Lots of well know entertainers / comedians started their career this way at similar events, a bit like the old concert party days.

All the acts were fully vetted prior to the big night we also had a full dress rehearsal. This was our London Palladium and I was asked to act as MC (*Master of Ceremonies*), for the evening. On this particular occasion I was actually selected, apparently my name was mentioned at a meeting due to my previous attempts at performing my comedy routine/set, in the corporals and sergeants mess earlier that year. I wasn't at the meeting but I imagine it went something like this:

<u>Battalion 2ic's Conference October 1982</u>: OK chaps the Christmas Revue is coming up soon and we need someone to act as MC for the evening, the rehearsals are in a few days, anyone got any suggestions? Rupert, Rodney, Charles, Tarquin, do you have anyone in mind? RSM what about you? I'm not fucking doing it ... No Mr Hunt do you have anyone in mind? Yes, young Corporal Mooney Sir, I saw him performing in the mess the other night he seems a confident little fucker, he's quite funny too. Mooney mmmm, do I know him, his name rings a bell? ... Ah yes the boxer fellow, I remember him, let's get him to do it, otherwise the Colonel said one of us has to do it... And that's how I got the gig, allegedly.

Although we had the dress rehearsal the only person who didn't get a chance to rehearse was yours truly, the main concern during the rehearsal was for the act's to practice and confirm the running order. I just stood there in my black suit and black bowtie announcing the acts. On the night of the show it was a completely different affair. I had to fill in during the natural breaks, to adlib was a slight understatement.

On the night of the show I decided to wear a black curly wig in addition to my black suit bowtie and red braces, and being from Oldham I was a natural at impersonating Bobby Ball of Cannon and Ball fame, the popular Lancashire comedy duo, who rose to fame in the late 70's and early 80's. I remained in character throughout the evening. I was no longer the Best Loser in the gym on that night. I felt completely comfortable on stage, it seemed so natural, an experience I had many times after that, and I loved the attention. Many members of the audience actually thought I was comedian booked to host the show, (*yes I was that good*). At one point I found myself signing autographs for the kids. A complete contrast to how I felt less than 12 months previous.

Looking back on this I can see why I enjoyed it, not only was I being noticed and remembered, I was being liked, but at the time I was unaware of how powerful this combination of the likeability factor was. Being liked was not something we normally associated within the realms of army philosophy. *'I'm not here to be liked lad, I'm here to get the job done"*. Was a phrase more a kin to the army philosophy at the time.

Likeability is quite a common word today, as many of us are familiar with TV shows like the X Factor or Britain's Got Talent, I'm a celebrity, Big brother, to name but a few. The likeability of a contestant plays a big part in who we choose as our favourite. We also seem to be living in a world of reality TV, where people seem desperate to attain this likeability, although quite often we tend to like the crazy ones too. Those that are voted off first are always the ones who seem to melt into the background almost going unnoticed. Which for some reason reminds me of a quote I once read in a book, by Ali Campbell, *"shy kids get no chocolate"*. The book is titled "Just Get On With It". In one of the chapters he talks about being in a meeting when he was a young man, he was a little shy at the time, and was procrastinating over something, not quite sure what to do, when one of his senior colleagues' said speak up son. Shy kids get no chocolate. In other words, stand up for yourself, challenge things, take control and don't just let life happen to you.

So those two nights of complete contrast, one where I became the likeable little chap from Oldham and the other were I was undoubtedly the BEST LOSER, helped to shape my military career. All in all, I went on to have a very successful 23 years in the Army, most of which is covered in this book. During this time I travelled all over the world, I was awarded the BEM, (British Empire Medal), promoted to WO1, RSM, (*Regimental Sergeant Major*). In the opinion of many people I had reached my ultimate goal. But that label I had given myself at the age of twenty one continued to haunt me later in life, especially when things weren't quite going the way I planned. At times I was still the "BEST LOSER" and one day I allowed it to completely destroy my confidence. The confidence I never seemed to have as a child, but the confidence that achievement brings, the confidence that comes with experience, the confidence that comes as a result of knowledge, it was gone. I allowed myself to slip back to the feeling of emptiness, losing myself in life's maze.

The following chapters of this book highlight the events that lead to this dark period in my life. How close I came to total self-destruction as a result of anxiety and depression. To where I am now and why I felt the need to write all this down. I started writing this book as reminder to myself of the things I had done and achieved, it was never really intended to be published. As my initial intention was to simply write down ten things that made me feel good about myself, as part of a self-help exercise, and something I had read somewhere. Many of the books I have read over the years or see on the shelves in bookshops are written by famous people/ celebrities who always seem to have a rags to riches story to tell.

This is not a rags to riches story, well not in the monetary sense, at times it may seem a little self-indulgent, it's difficult not to be when writing about yourself. The first few chapters cover the period that lead to my breakdown, with flashbacks to other key areas that I believe helped to shape the person I became. As you read through it please be aware that although this may seem to follow the conventional autobiography style, my overall aim was to help me find a way out, a way out from my constant feeling of failure.

Chapter 2

New Beginnings

I left the army with mixed emotions; I could have stayed on until at least the age of 55 if I really wanted to. Deep down I wanted to take that risk, try something new, start again, find success in the real world. (*Whatever the real world was?*)

That little voice inside my head was telling me it was time to leave. Perhaps this voice was that of my long suffering wife Linda, who up until this moment I have not yet mentioned, the beautiful girl I first met on a 404 bus in Oldham in June 1975. The girl who I then married at the age of 19, on the 7th of July 1979. The wife who gave us three fantastic sons, the wife who supported me throughout my army career, without question. Allowing me to fulfil my ambition. She was pleased I was leaving, it's fair to say that she was fucking overjoyed, *her words not mine*, but she made it clear it was my decision.

It was the year of the new millennium and at the age of 40 it was the prime time to step out and try something completely different. As part of my transition to this so called real world of commerce and industry I discovered the subject of Marketing and set out to complete my degree before completing my military service which was due to end in mid-April 2000.

Although the Army and other armed services support you in the transition, you still have a job to do, and after 20 plus years of loyal services you often feel obliged to focus more on your current military job, commitments, and responsibilities, than those that are critical to your future... in short like many ex-servicemen I did not find the time to use the full quota of resettlement. I never finished my degree, something I later regretted.

I actually started studying marketing three years prior to leaving the Army and despite being posted to Newcastle to work with the Universities for my last two years, (*the perfect opportunity and environment*). I still never found or made time to complete this degree. I did however gain a great knowledge in web design, (*but more on that later*).

When the day of leaving finally came we packed up our house in Newcastle, a private married quarter, a beautiful large four bed roomed detached house we had lived in for the past two years. It was a relief for my wife; she was pleased to be moving back to our own house in Tameside. Fortunately we had bought this house some years earlier. At least we had the experience of paying a mortgage for the past 11 years. Unlike many servicemen who tend to leave this to the final hour, and although living in a married quarter is not free you do have to pay rent, however having a commitment of a mortgage is a completely new ball game to some.

Our other reason for moving back would mean the lads would be returning to an area they were more familiar with and family was just around the corner. (*Just a figure of speech*), they lived close by within a fifteen mile radius, give or take a few miles.

The first three years after leaving the Army were exciting; with the initial security of having a pot of money and a monthly pension meant that we had little to worry about as far as money was concerned. With almost £50,000 pounds in the bank and a regular pension, things were great. Looking back though there was so much more I could have done with that investment. (*More on that later*).

During the first year I set about the task of building a business. I decided that I wanted to do all the things I loved doing while serving in the army.

My real passion was training/teaching. I suppose I enjoyed standing at the front of the class, for me there is no better job satisfaction than being in a position to influence others, either by your knowledge of a particular subject or by the way you interact with them, which undoubtedly results in them feeding from it. Or was it simply that I just loved the sound of my own voice? Maybe it was that hidden performer in me constantly trying to get out. Whatever it was I had a hungry passion for it.

So in May 2000 I registered myself as self-employed, and although I have a lot of respect for my fellow servicemen and women, I was adamant I was not going to fall into the stereotypical job of police, prison service or some other security based employment often associated with ex-servicemen and women.

Perhaps it was the study of marketing that propelled me on this particular path, as I was becoming more commercially aware. Deep down I wanted to make money, as I thought that if I could make it to my first million it would mean that I had succeeded in the real world. Yes I was naive

My initial long term goal I set myself was to be in a position to retire at the age of 55, or at least be totally financially independent. At the time of writing this particular chapter I am still more than a million miles from this objective, as I am now almost 53, that initial 15 year goal is fast approaching. My first attempt at starting a business went quite well in my opinion, (*well initially*). But first let me give you a little background on how I arrived at my business plan.

Prior to leaving the army while serving in Northern Ireland as an RQMS (*Regimental Quartermaster Sergeant*), means nothing to most of you I am sure, and I am almost sure you don't want me to bore you with a full job description here, but humour me, I'll try to be quick.

One of my many commitments meant I was responsible for the maintenance and security of the computer equipment (*when I say maintenance I mean sending them away to be fixed, not fixing them myself*), these computers where housed in the Interactive Learning Centre, yes the army had its finger on the pulse on this one back in 1996. This added responsibility lead to my interest in computers, i.e. the front end, basically I found myself sat behind a screen most evenings, learning all the Microsoft applications, Word, Excel, Access, PowerPoint. Most of the time I found that I spent more time showing others than doing my own stuff. Then in my final post/job, as a Regimental Sergeant Major

I found myself also teaching PowerPoint and presentation skills to university students at the OTC (*Officer Training Corps*) in Newcastle, as many of these students had a real interest in using PowerPoint for their dissertation. So basically this new found knowledge was the basis on which my business was going to be based. It was also during this time when I was first introduced to the subject of web design and domain names. And in 1999 I registered my first domain names, and set up my first website.

To add a little more substance to how I arrived at my first business plan, was that in 2000 local councils also setup similar Interactive Learning Centres in the towns close to where I lived. This was part of the drive to get adults interested in using computers. I visited a few of them as part of my initial research, manly with a view of working in one of them. Although my many years of experience as an instructor and trainer, not to mention my knowledge of the very same computer applications they were teaching meant nothing, as I had no formal civilian qualifications to hang my hat on. Experience in this case counted for nothing; sometimes you need little pieces of paper. (*Mention the army to some people and their eyes glaze over, especially within the world of academia*). For the next five years I never actually mentioned to anyone that I was an ex-serviceman.

So a week after leaving the army I decide it was time to go back to college and get my pieces of paper. I enrolled on the Microsoft Office User Specialist courses at MANCAT (*Manchester College of Arts and Technology*), and spent a number of weeks getting certified for all the main applications.

This was actually FREE at the time, as businesses were getting support for their employees to attend the courses. I was self-employed so I was technically both an employer and employee; all I need was a business card and letterhead to secure my place on the courses. My Photoshop skills came in handy, as I created my own artwork for my logo, letterhead and compliment slips, creating the identity for my new business name TEACH U2.

It was also at this time when I registered my business with a local Business Enterprise, and gained additional knowledge in the rudiments of running a business. I was pointed in the right direction and gained valuable assistance with both my Marketing & Business Plan. Within a few weeks I also had in place all the necessary business insurance, liability cover, I also registered with Data Protection, opened a new business account, and I was ready to officially start trading. During the first few months I spent over two thousand pounds on advertising my new business in both the Thompson Directory and Yellow pages. I asked them to place my ad in the computer tuition section and was promptly told that they did not have a section for computer tuition so my ads were placed in the computer service section. Guess what the phone never rang. Tell a lie, it did once, when someone asked if I sold monitors. All the other calls were from people wanting to sell me more advertising. I made the classic mistake of waiting for the phone to ring.

The big ads were not working for me so I placed a small ad in the Local Advertiser one of those free papers, guess what, the phone started to ring. I found that all my clients were over 40's, my eldest client was in his 80's, I found my demographic. These were the people who felt intimidated by going to a class, the people who said they would be embarrassed sitting with others who they thought would know more than them.

I found my niche, I was teaching basic computer skills, everything from switching it on to creating and sending email, using a scanner, setting up printers, basically everything you need to know to get you up and running. As the first year went on I found that I was teaching a whole range of different adult students, all with mixed abilities and varying levels of computer literacy. One of my clients was a lady in her 60's who recently suffered a stroke, and found that using the keyboard and mouse was great therapy. I was working around the clock, if I wasn't out with a client, I was sat at my computer in my converted garage, (*my home office/command centre*), learning something new, I was hungry for knowledge.

Having spent all of my previous working life getting paid month after month and not even thinking about it, with the money just being there at the end of the month. It was a real buzz when someone handed over hard cash, after sitting with them for over two hours, helping them solve a problem or learn something new, it was a great feeling. The problem I had was that my initial plan was limited to the amount of money I could make.

At the time I was only charging £25.00 to £30.00 per hour, and spent approximately two hrs with each client.

Most days I was seeing on average three clients sometimes four a day. Resulting in a £90.00 to £110.00 a day income, and working 5 days a week wasn't too bad a wage in the year 2000, especially when topped up with my army pension.

The problem I faced was this wasn't a millionaire plan, OK I could make a living, but as I saw it there was very little chance of it making a million. I had this obsession that a million pounds meant success, something had to change.

So what changed?

Chapter 3

Making a Million

While I was doing all this stuff I was also tinkering on the Internet, exploring other ways to make money. It was long before the time of broadband and using a dial up connection meant things were much, much slower than they are today. It was a time when local businesses were showing the first real signs in advertising on the web, at this time I also discovered Affiliate Marketing, but more on that later. *I say that a lot in this book. I suppose that's the procrastinator in me.*

My real interest now was finding out how I could increase my leverage on time, we all get 24hrs to play with so what could I do in this time that resulted in a constant return. Basically I wanted to find a way to provide a service that I only had to do once and constantly get paid for. I needed to find something to do when I was not sat with a client from my TEACH U2 business.

Creating an online business directory was the option I went for. My basic plan was to charge a fee for setting up an individual web page for each business, publishing it to an online directory. At the time most other directories consisted of simply a name and address format and included everyone and anyone regardless of the quality. Also at the time there were no online directories that covered Greater Manchester, well none that covered all ten districts on one single website. Obviously it's a little different now.

To create my directory I literally spent two years walking around the high streets and industrial estates looking for businesses, ones that caught my eye, seeking out businesses I would gladly be happy to do business with myself, good real down to earth hard working folk. Particularly those that seemed to stand out from the rest, basically my aim was to seek out quality not quantity. At the time I had nothing to sell I was offering my directory service for FREE. Understandably some responses I got were negative, the old cry of *"we don't need to advertise we already have a referral system"*, or all our business comes from recommendations, however many more were positive. Its funny looking back that the vast majority of negative people I met are no longer in business.

It was a real learning curve. It's also surprising what business owners will tell you, I learnt a lot just listening to them. I also built up some great friendships along the way too. The best thing was discovering that lots of these business owners were ideal clients for my teaching business. Some just needing help with setting up spreadsheets, mail merge or wanted to know how they setup their own website and email addresses. Today it's all aspects of social media and content management… but let's not digress eh.

So this was basic marketing, I went in offering something for free and indirectly found out what it was they really needed. Marketing is all about discovering and anticipating the wants and needs of your potential customers. Turn something that they want into something they now need, supply it to them at a profit and you can't fail to make money.

So let's get back to the plan… Greater Manchester is made up of 10 Districts these are Wigan, Bolton, Bury, Rochdale, Oldham, Tameside, Stockport, Manchester, Trafford and Salford. OK did I really have to name them all? *(But you never know when questions like this will come in handy, "name the ten districts that make up Greater Manchester?")* Now you know.

My aim was to have a minimum of 1000 businesses listed from each of the ten districts, ten thousand businesses, all paying me a minimum of £100.00 per year. Quite simply that would give a turnover of 1 million. *(Just for the record some businesses actually paid me £500.00 per year)*. It was a simple plan on paper, and I set myself a two year objective to achieve this. Basically I needed to list at least 10 businesses per day on the directory. Remember I was initially offering this service for free, with a view to charging them at a later date, once the website was more established. It seemed all so easy on paper… things always are. Funny thing was… it did work and many of these businesses started to see real benefits, so naturally within a few months they paid me. I finally had another business, "Have a Link" was born, and another source of income was added to my portfolio.

So in less than 12 months I had two business ideas, both feeding each other. I was walking into businesses cold, simply asking if they wanted to be included on the directory, remember there was no hard sell here, it was free. I wasn't some commission hungry salesman desperate to make a sale.

Many asked what was the catch, nothing is free right? I just said I would return in 3 or 4 months to show them how effective this type of promotion can be, I said I can email you the results, just give me your email address. (*My all-important email list was gathering pace*). Some actually said we don't use email we've got a FAX Machine why do we need email? Some of these businesses needed real help. If they passed me their email address and it was, whoever@aol.com or @freeserve.com or some other Mickey Mouse address. I would ask why they did not have an email generic to their business name... a common reply was, "*how do we do that*" I simply said, "I can TEACH U2". I didn't actually say that but I'm sure you know what I mean here. You can now see how the two businesses worked together.

The classic mistake I was making was that I was running before learning to walk. I was working 24/7, now don't get me wrong I was making money, good money, but due to my commitments and self-imposed pressure I put on myself, those all-important little tasked of running a business were not being done. The tasks that will eventually come back and bite you on the arse... TAX, VAT, ACCOUNTS! They were the things you can put off until the weekend right? The trouble was that weekend didn't come round often enough. I paid the price for this as you will find out later.

My business model was growing, and by the end of my third year I was now offering a complete marketing service. I teamed up with a graphics design business and moved in with them to share an office at a business centre in Saddleworth. It was an additional financial commitment but this added another string to my bow. I was now also in the print brokering business. On advice from my accountant I decided to go Limited (*still not sure why I did this*), but hey my business cards now said Managing Director… whoopee do eh. What I didn't know at this time was that it also brought a whole host of other commitments. I was now into the realms of Corporation Tax, quarterly and annual returns, VAT and Tax returns. If these aren't done correctly you pay the price, don't get me wrong here I did have an accountant who was looking after this side of the business, but they can only work with what you give them. My problem was I had a tendency to leave all this stuff to the last minute. I was far too busy with the real stuff, getting more clients, keeping the ones I already had happy, looking for new products to add to my growing portfolio of services. Accounts, bookkeeping was always something I could do later. I bet you can guess where this is going?

By the end of 2004 I decided to stop the TEACH U2 side of my business and focus on the directory, it was at this time that Google introduced its Google AdSense program to their portfolio. If you are not familiar with this, it's basically a system where you place a snippet of code on your web pages which then displays ads on your content, when these ads are clicked you get paid a small fee. Therefore if you have a website that's getting a reasonable amount of traffic you can make a significant fee from Google.

I spent months pasting this code manually into all my web pages, it was no doubt time consuming compared to how you can do it today; however it paid off, and after a few months I was making on average £600 to £700 additional profit per month just from these ads alone. It was also at this time when I discovered Affiliate Marketing. Once again if you are not familiar with this process I'll explain the basics. In outline you build web based content, promote other businesses products on your website i.e. consumer products and when a visitor from your website clicks through to the merchant site and buys the product you get a fee based on a percentage commission. One of the websites I built generated in excess of £1000.00 pounds per day in commission sales.

I now had three residual streams of income on my directory website alone, money from the businesses that advertised and paid annually, also money from Google AdSense, plus Affiliate Commissions. I now had a number of fully functioning monetised websites, generating a substantial income, I had finally worked out how to leverage my time. Just imagine what I could do if I had a few staff to assist me? It was time to look for an investor; this was a potential gold mine.

The winner of The Apprentice in 2014 went to Sir Alan with a very similar business proposition to the one I was now working on. Does this mean I was 10 years ahead of my time…?

Chapter 4

Making a BIG Mistake

It was now 2005 I was five years into my fifteen year plan to become financially independent, debt free, living the life of total satisfaction. I was more positive than ever. I rewrote my business plan, as this was now totally focused on the directory business and print brokering; it was a plausible plan for any would-be investor.

The Law of Attraction in Action: A local successful businessman who was also an existing client and the Managing Director of one of the first businesses I added to my directory had watched me grow over the years. He saw my enthusiasm and drive during those early years, and in time we became good friends. I did quite a lot of promotional work for him during that five year period, we often chatted about business and marketing. He was in a way a mentor to me. I had watched with great interest what he did with his business over the past five years and learned so much from him. We got together in June that year and discussed the future of the directory; he was impressed with what I showed him and he couldn't believe I was doing all this myself. The investment I original asked for was a little ambitious, and being a shrewd businessman he had his own ideas on how he could help me. I believe he wanted to see for himself what this business could do.

He had a spare office in a building he bought recently, I say office; this building was more like a large warehouse with offices above it. He offered to let me use this space rent free and initially invested £5000 to help offset the cost of new computers furniture and get the phone lines and broadband up and running. In addition to this he also gave me two of his female staff to assist with admin and office duties; they also remained on his payroll, as this would mean that I was not committed to their salaries and PAYE, plus all the additional headaches that can bring… I also took on a freelance salesman and graphic designer. The team was now in place, we were ready to go.

Before I embarked on this new phase I took a brief ten day working holiday to Turkey with Linda as a belated 25th silver wedding anniversary break; something we had been planning for a few months, we had not been away together since…. Err, actually this was the first time we had been away on our own since our Honeymoon in 1979, when we spent four days in Llandudno, it was going to be seven days but my new bride was ill so we cut the break short. Only to find out that we weren't quite alone after all, as the sickness she was suffering was the effects of morning sickness, Linda was pregnant with our first born. So this holiday in Turkey was in effect our honeymoon, if this isn't procrastination I don't not what is, *"but more on that later"*. I called this a working holiday because the place where we were staying was owned by a client of mine. I had recently finished building a website for her and her partner, which sole purpose was to promote their Luxury Villa online. So both Linda and I were invited to take a holiday there to test that all the systems worked, everything from being met at the airport to hiring a car, going on day trips and checking out the local restaurants. (*This is what you call a working holiday.*)

This was a chance for us both to re-charge our batteries, get away from it all. When I returned I was firing on all cylinders, simply buzzing on what the future was going to hold. I am sure you have experienced this yourself, that feeling of anticipation and excitement, that first day back at school after the six week holidays, (*ok perhaps not that excited*). Christmas Eve when you are seven years old, and you still believe Santa is real. (*That kind of excitement*).

I moved into my new offices on Monday 18th July 2005 and sat down with my new team, gave them lists of a few thousand emails, telephone numbers and business addresses, this wasn't some dodgy list you can buy on the internet this was a qualified list of business contacts I had built up over the years. These were all the businesses that had contacted me or I had previously been to see personally, all qualified leads, it was time to get cracking and start converting.

Things seemed to be going well at first as I could now concentrate on running the business instead of doing everything myself. On paper we were looking good. I could now also implement my plan of selling excess stock on eBay. This was another idea I had which involved selling excess stock and new lines from local businesses, all of which were already clients on the directory. Many of these being mainly independent clothing retail outlets, who I'd already primed for this service during my recent visits, in addition to these we also sold Garden Speakers, Coffee Pots and the latest in two wheel Skateboards which we had a lot of fun on, skating round the warehouse.

At this time eBay was becoming popular for many businesses, although many did not have the time and in most cases the know-how of how to do this themselves. So in effect I acted as a trading assistant for them, this became a very popular service and was already successful in the US. The general idea was to sell the stock and take a 22% cut of the sale value, plus the cost of the listing fees incurred. The new warehouse space meant that I could now store their products and dispatch in house. This was an attractive offer to businesses as it meant that not only were we selling their stock we were also freeing up valuable storage space. So what went wrong?

If I told you that we now had sales on eBay each day in excess of £1000.00, plus the sales from the directory averaging 10 per week and affiliate commissions, not to mention the occasional print job, what could be going wrong? Was I not sitting on a gold mine?

After just two months the salesman left us, he found it hard to convert the businesses, and meet the quota. It wasn't that he was a bad salesman, he had been recommended; he just wasn't internet savvy. Therefore he met some difficulties when faced with those business owners who knew just that little bit more than him. Obviously it was easy for me to sell this concept, it was my baby and I knew it inside out. I had all the answers to deflect any negative comments from would-be clients, and could back up any claims with real confidence.

So I put myself back on the frontline rather than getting another salesperson, (*Mistake No1*). I was too attached to my business, (*Mistake No2*). The staff who were originally employed to call clients, arrange appointments and update the listings were finding themselves dealing with the huge admin tail I'd created by being a Powerseller / Trading Assistant on eBay, (*Mistake No3*).

Although it would be another two years before it all started crashing down around me it was still an exciting time. My work load had increased, it wasn't that I failed to delegate, I just couldn't let go completely, and my big problem was the directory. I now had other people listing but found myself constantly correcting work. I found myself sat at home in my office late into the night, going over what had been done that day, with that thought inside my head, one that we have all heard more than a thousand times before **"if a job's worth doing it's worth doing well"** my problem was, that like many of you I'm sure, I changed this well know phrase to **"if a job is worth doing right, do it yourself"** (*Mistake No4*). This meant that the important stuff which was my sole responsibility was now being neglected, this can be summed up in one word "ACCOUNTS". (*Mistake No5*). The money was coming in but it was also going out, the Taxman was jumping all over me. When the late penalty fines came I just paid them rather than sort out the problem, as it was much easier, because it meant the problem went away for a while, even though I was paying out much more than it would have cost me, as I found out much later. I just wanted them off my back. My head was well and truly buried in the sand on this one.

Until one day I got a knock at the door and was greeted by a tall slim looking woman, who was very smartly dressed and accompanied by a tall smart gentleman dressed in a long overcoat, dark suit and shiny black shoes; both had folders under their arms. Before they said a word I just knew they had not come to sell me anything, or tell me I had just won the lottery. If you have ever met members of the Inland Revenue you will know what I mean.

The lady spoke to ask if she could speak to Mr Mooney I was promptly handed a business card that said they were from the "Hidden Economy Team" it was one of those moments when someone is speaking to you and you are just not listening, you just focus on one thing, "Hidden Economy" what the fuck? I could see her lips moving, I was just nodding, and all kinds of thoughts immediately entered my head. I was about to be investigated by Moulder and Scully, I was in my own X Files nightmare. All I remember saying at the time was that I was moving my business back home and that all my accounts, books and files where there, I had nothing to hide and they could gladly come and take a look. In less than an hour we were all sat in my office at home, I handed them all my arch leaver files containing my invoices, job sheets, PayPal sales, the lot. Like I said I had nothing to hide.

I wasn't a complete buffoon, although I said I often failed on my accounting it's not that I didn't know what to do. I was actually more than qualified, I was very meticulous I filed all my receipts, actually I kept good records, I just failed when it came to completing returns on-time. After the initial inspection I was asked to logon to my PayPal account and show my history of earnings, they wanted to see the last two years accounts. These can take some time to download, so I was told that the lady would return in two weeks' time to complete the report.

That two weeks came round pretty quick, however I had everything laid out in order when she returned, she thanked me on a well presented set of accounts she went through all the invoices, job sheets PayPal figures, like a school teacher marking reports, in less than an hour she told me that her report and findings will be sent to me in a week or so, she tucked her folder under her arm shook my hand and left. A week later that distinctive brown envelope arrived, my heart was racing, and I had a feeling that this was not going to be good news. Basically I was informed that I had not paid VAT to the sum of £15,000 and had seven days in which to pay. That cold sweat, the feeling of panic, where you find yourself walking back and forth not really knowing why or what you are doing, before you sit down and put you head in your hands to try and think your way out of this one. That first thought is that this must be wrong? VAT at the time was at 17.5% there was no way I made over £100,000 certainly not as a profit. I worked out that she had not taken into account the money I had paid out to the businesses I was selling the stock for; I believe that she had also mixed some of the job sheets with invoices. I found myself staring at the phone, eventually I phoned the number on top of the letter, and was finally directed to some guy in Liverpool, not before jumping through a few hoops first. After a lengthy

Making a BIG Mistake

conversation he agreed that I could pay instalments of £2000.00 per month until such time as this matter was rectified.

Finding that £2000.00 each month was crippling me. Not long after that the building I had been working from was now being sold by my long time business friend, the new owners agreed that I could remain there but needed to pay rent, all the money I was now making from this business was now being paid out. I was personally earning ZERO, not one single penny. I soldiered on thinking that things will get better; it was a long time coming. The new owners completely renovated the warehouse turning it into new smaller units, we moved around in-between the building work, at times the noise was unbearable. On completion more businesses moved in and things started to look up, until one morning just two weeks before Christmas, we arrived to the sight of police lots of broken glass, yes we had all been robbed. We had operated there quietly for almost two years and now as soon as the other businesses moved in, it was all gone, apart from a couple of computers. I was devastated, that best loser feeling was there once more. I managed to keep things going for another 8-9 months. Until I got a call from my sister on Friday afternoon on the 17th August, 2007. My mum had been rushed to Oldham Royal with breathing problems; it was the start of the weekend that would change my life forever.

Chapter 5

Unbelievable

My mum being admitted to hospital was nothing new; we had almost come to expect it over the last few years. She had suffered with breathing problems for many years now and was on permanent oxygen, so this call was not out of the ordinary. She was admitted many times before; however this time was different, I never rushed to get there before I normally went in the evening during normal visiting hours. This time I left as soon as I hung up the phone. I had a strange feeling in my stomach. When I arrived she was still in A & E sat upright on a trolley while a male nurse was struggling to fit what I can only describe as a full face respirator, it was clear he was having problems. My mum just looked at me and I could see in her eyes that this was different to all the other times she had been admitted. The male nurse disappeared to seek advice on how to fit the respirator. We all just looked at each other and seemed to stand there in silence. Both my sister and Stepdad said very little apart from the odd break in silence when he said you'll be alright Mag. I think he was the only one who thought that this was just like all the other times when she was admitted.

After a few hours of standing around wondering what was going on, we were directed to the waiting room of the High Dependency Unit, then after a long wait we were finally called to the family room, and told that my mother would not be resuscitated if she got into further difficulties, my Stepdad still seemed totally oblivious to what was going to happen. It was now just after midnight both me and my sister stayed while all the others left to get some rest. We both took turns sitting with our mum throughout the night; at times she was quite chatty but kept drifting off, we spoke about my dad as she would often do when we were alone, she still loved him and missed him since that night when he was taken from us in 1974. The coroner's report said that he died of a brain haemorrhage as a result of a fall down a fire escape at a night club in Oldham, something I will cover in a later chapter

This was real quality time with my mum. I felt a mixture of guilt for not seeing her more often despite the fact that she lived just less than five miles away; nevertheless I was also pleased that I could spend this time with her. This was without doubt the most precious time you can spend with someone you love especially your mum. It was strange but I had an unusual feeling that she was not yet quite ready to go, although her breathing was a struggle, her heart was pounding. She would often squeeze my hand, she felt strong, and it was as if she would let me know when it was time.

She asked me how Mick was. Mick is my elder brother Michael who suffered a major brain haemorrhage, once back in 1976, when he was just eighteen, his second when he was 32. During both these times I was still serving in the Army, the first time I was just a young 16 year old boy soldier when the call came, and was granted compassionate leave to go home and see him. I travelled all the way from Folkestone to Oldham, it was a journey that seemed to take forever, not knowing what I would be facing when I got there. At sixteen I just knew that a brain haemorrhages was serious stuff, the same injury that caused my dad's death. Fortunately Mick was fit and well enough and survived unscathed, or so we thought.

When he had this second major bleed I was fortunately serving locally as a Staff Instructor with the TA (*Territorial Army*) in Tameside. This meant that I was close enough to be there almost immediately when the call came from his wife Michelle, to tell me that he had been admitted to Crumpsall Hospital in Manchester. Once again I found myself in a family room this time it was just me and his wife who took the news, this was a serious bleed, what we didn't know was that Mick had three weak areas on his brain which apparently he had since the first bleed all those years ago. One had bust, and unlike before were it was easy to stop, this was not as simple because stopping this bleed would mean that there would now be more pressure on the other weak areas, and he was going to be lucky if he survived the operation. Before he went down to theatre I sat with him, he was fully conscious and told me not to leave him, we hugged each other and I told him that everything was going to be OK and I would be waiting for him when he returned. When they wheeled him away I was left with a feeling of helplessness, one that I had only experienced one time before, a time when there is nothing you can do to prevent the outcome. It was a long three hour operation to stop the bleed.

When he returned I was shocked to see that his head was now completely shaved, he had staples running from one ear to the other, his head was now almost twice the size. There was a tube running from one side of his head to a bottle to drain off fluid/blood. He was now in an induced coma and things where looking pretty grim. I held his hand and felt a very slight squeeze the type you get from a young baby when you place your finger on its open palm. I sat with him for a few hours before returning home to give my sister and younger brother the news.

That night I lay in bed with my wife and sobbed uncontrollably. This was something I had never ever done before, and for the first time in all the years I had been married I totally opened up and told her that I felt completely helpless. As this was a feeling I once had on the streets of Northern Ireland, when I watched two men dying in front of me, they had both been shot in the head. Just three hours earlier I was drinking coffee with them. (*Something I will cover in a later chapter*). There was nothing I could do to prevent it and I felt that same feeling of helplessness while sitting at my brothers bedside just before he went down to theatre, telling him that everything was going to be OK but knowing that I was completely helpless. Only to see him return the way he did. I was the lucky one with a wife to wrap her arms around me, to give me that reassurance that everything was going to be fine.

For the next twelve months I went to the hospital every day, not knowing what the long term effects were going to be, would he ever speak or walk again, the doctors could tell us nothing. He had suffered a major brain trauma, some people never recover. During the first few weeks after he regained consciousness I started taking in photographs of when we were kids growing up. Although he could not speak at this stage and was paralysed down his left side, similar to that associated with stroke victims; he did however start to gain use of his right hand. I was desperate to know if he actually remembered us. One particular picture I kept showing him was of the four of us, it still hangs in my office today, a small old black and white picture of me our Mick, my younger brother Patrick (Paddy) and my dad. I was about seven years old, Mick was nine and Paddy was three. I kept pointing to our dad in the picture and asked if he knew who that was, I placed a pen in his hand and indicted to him to write on my hand, he almost broke my skin constantly writing a large D on my hand. This was a real breakthrough and eventually after a few more weeks he was writing yes and no on a note pad. This went on for months, although we were still none the wiser on how much damage to his brain he had suffered. He still wasn't speaking and unable to walk or use his left hand. I was beginning to wonder if this was it, there was also the worry that he was still faced with these other weak areas on his brain. Despite having a brain shunt, a procedure that relieves pressure in the brain by draining fluids to the abdomen via a tube just under his skin.

He was still quite vulnerable; although there were signs that he was getting better albeit slight. On one particular visit the guy in the next bed said that Mick spoke today, the guy said he was looking out of the window and said *"it's a nice day today Mick*" and Mick replied "*is it*" that's all he said nothing more. I looked at Mick in anticipation waiting for him to speak to me but all I ever got from him was strange facial movements, similar to when you try to force air out of your mouth while your lips are tightly shut. I said come on you tosser (*a word we often used to show disappointment, this was a word Mick used quite often*), speak to me, but nothing, just these strange facial contortions. A few weeks past and while I was at work I received a phone call one afternoon from Mick's wife, she just said I've got someone here who wants to speak to you.

What I'm about to write next sounds like a scene from a film, it's unbelievable but I swear it's very true.

Michelle was pushing Mick in a wheelchair down the corridor in the hospital and as they passed the Payphone on the wall he put his hand on the wheel to stop it. Until this point Mick had never spoken since that first time when all he said was "*is it*" she just asked him if he wanted to call somebody, she heard him say YES!, she turned him to face the Payphone, the next thing was quite amazing and the first truly unbelievable moment in this chapter. Although he had very little movement in his left arm as it was still bent and resting on his chest, his right arm was now fully functional, he just reached up, grabbed the receiver in his right hand and with his index finger he punched in my number on the keypad. This was the first real sign that he was remembering stuff, Michelle at that point took the phone off him as she just couldn't believe what she had just seen. When I answered she gave the phone back to Mick, this is how that call went.

"Is that you Mick" nothing no reply, Mick is that you? ... Yes,

I was shaking with excitement "how you do-in" again there was a long pause before he replied,

"I'm fine I'm in a fucking wheelchair, how are you",

"I'm great Mick, are you going to talk to me when I get there tonight" there was another pause before he replied,

"yes course I will"

"don't let me down Mick, I love you, you tosser, you had better speak to me when I get there tonight…

"I will".

That night we all arrived in anticipation, Mick was in bed during visiting time, I just stood at the end of his bed looked at him and said come-on then talk to us you tosser, once again all we got were the same strange facial contortions, no sound, no words, nothing. My mum looked at me as if I had made it all up. I just sat there thinking what you playing at Mick you're making me look like a right pratt here. That night I was the last to leave, I leant over to his ear and said in a whisper *"why didn't you speak to me don't you know I love you, you tosser"*, after a short pause I heard him say *"I love you too, you tosser"*. Tears were once again streaming down my face; I just stood up looked at him and smiled the biggest smile. It dawned on me that when we were looking at him he was trying to speak and nothing was happening, it's as if his brain was telling him he was speaking but all that was happening were the facial contortions. When the guy in the next bed first said "it's a nice day today" he was looking out of the window and not at Mick, when he was on the payphone to me he was looking at the wall with his wife behind him. And when I finally bent down to say goodnight and to tell him that I loved him I was not looking him in the eye. The long pauses meant that he was trying and he was probably making the same facial contortions but no one could see him… all I can say at this point is, it's unbelievable, but I can assure you this is true.

I continued to visit him every day until my posting ended when I was once again found myself serving in Northern Ireland.

Although Mick never made a full recovery to where he was before this accident and despite having a major relapse just a few weeks after this unbelievable incident, he battled on and is still with us today. Unfortunately it was all too much for his young wife Michelle, she was only 24 when this happened to Mick and it was a lot for a young mother to deal with, they later got divorced. Mick now lives in a residential home in Rochdale, he still suffers short term memory loss, and has difficulty breathing, and requires constant care. I try to see him as often as I can, *(which I know is not enough, I need to make more effort)*.

That morning after spending quality time with our mum both me and my sister went to break the news to Mick. We drove to Rochdale to collect him, although at the time it's was 16 years on from his accident, it's still hard to fully understand the extent of damage this bleed caused to his brain. At times he just seems to be in a world of his own, you can hold short conversations with him and he appears to remember everything from his past, especially when we were growing up. But how would he react to seeing our mum clearly reaching the end, it was hard to say. We decided to just tell him that she was seriously ill in hospital and did he want to come with us to see her, naturally he did. That afternoon my mum had all the family together, sitting and standing by the bed.

The nurse asked if we were religious, we had all been brought up catholic, went to catholic schools had communion, were confirmed, although none of us were now regular church goes, we thought it only right that mum should be visited by a priest. The ward nurse said that she would call the duty padre to give my mum the last rights. It was now late in the afternoon on Saturday 18th August 2007, my sister said *"do you know what day it is today"*, naturally I said no, go on tell me, *"Its mums wedding anniversary,* she would have been married to my dad for 50 years today", no way that's unbelievable, that word was starting to be used more often. Things got a lot spookier after that.

I was standing in the corridor when the priest arrived, I shook his hand as I introduced myself, and asked him which parish he from... *"I'm father Derrick from St Anne's Church in Greenacres".* I was just dumbstruck by his reply and said nothing more to him. I could feel the tears welling up, but held back the emotion, we just walked to the room where mum was. I just stood there in silence with the others while he read my mum the last rights at 4.00pm that Saturday afternoon. When the short service was over I told my sister that the priest was from St Anne's, we both hugged each other. My mum had just been given the last rights by a priest from the same Church my mum and dad were married in over 50 years ago, on the 18th August at 4.00pm, totally unbelievable.

Understandably at this time we are more receptive to what is going on around us, anyone who as ever faced losing your mum will no doubt know what I mean, after the service we all knew that she didn't have long left, but it seemed like some kind of freak show as if we were all waiting and watching this poor woman die. I was starting to feel a little angry in a strange kind of way, I just found myself looking at my mum, she was drifting in and out of consciousness, but I got the feeling that she was thinking I'll make the buggers wait. As the evening approached some of the relatives left, I just knew she wasn't quite ready to go just yet.

By late evening there was just six of us sat around the bed. It seemed a little strange; it was as if we had been chosen to be there to experience something wonderful. That's probably a bizarre statement to make at a time like this, but for me watching my mum finally pass over was one of the most beautiful, while at the same time one of the saddest things I have ever seen. We sat there all night taking turns just holding her hand. Sitting on opposite sides of the bed, me and my sister and niece on one side, my stepdad, Dylis and her son Lee on the other.

As the night moved on I felt quite hot and asked the staff nurse if I could have some wet wipes so I could go and freshen up, my feet were on fire and it felt as though my shoes were filling with water. I walked down the corridor to the rest room and took my shoes and socks off to freshen my feet. I was just putting my socks back on when I had a strange feeling like a sharp tug on my arm as if my mum was saying come on, hurry up you little sod, I'm going now. I quickly powdered my feet put my socks and shoes on rushed back down the corridor. I sat in the chair next to my mum, it was now about 3.30am on Sunday Morning 19th August 2007. Her bed was next to door which was now open as it was quite warm in the room.

As you can imagine we were all tired and sometimes it's possible that during such a time what I am about to tell you can be explained as your mind playing tricks.

Personally I don't think so, because while I was sitting there I was just looking down at my mums hand, she still had a tight grip on mine, I was completely awake and had a feeling that someone had just opened the door and walked in, then stood at the end of my mums bed, although the door was already open. I'm not saying that I saw a ghost but I most certainly felt a presence, it was as though someone was stood between the gap from the wall to the head of the bed. At first I dismissed this as some kind of hallucination. I looked at my sister who was sat next to me, I didn't say anything but wanted to see if she had the same feeling, she just give me that look back that says "what?" without actually saying it. A few moments past and the same thing happened again, it then happened a third time, I thought my mind was playing tricks on me, but this was something I have never felt before. I could clearly feel the presence of three people stood behind my mum's bed. We often hear that when our time comes we are guided to spirit world by well-known faces from our past, (*I know this sounds a little crazy*).

I believe that my dad had come to guide her, along with his two closest brothers Mark and Thomas. These where the two uncles on my dad's side of the family who we had grown closest to when we were kids growing up, and naturally my dad had named me after them. So I suppose we always had a real connection. Just a few minutes later I stood up went to the end of mums bed kissed her on the forehead and said you can go now mum; it was as if I was now orchestrating the whole thing. I said to my sister, "Sharon mums going now, give her a kiss", and in turn as if in some kind of planned order I called each of them forward as the other sat down, finally to my stepdad who then just kissed her on the cheek, I said "no Gerald she wants a proper kiss", he then kissed her on the lips and said goodnight Mag, her hand seemed to fall from the bed onto his lap. I looked down at her face and that distinctive wash of peace made its way from her forehead over her face as if it was removing all the wrinkles, the pain, a lifetime of worries, and she was gone.

My mum passed away at 4.00am on Sunday 19th of August 2007. Understandably when we are faced with something like this our emotions are running high, I had not slept properly for three days, and I know this sounds a little bit crazy but to this day I believe that my dad, my uncle Mark and uncle Tom came for my mum that morning, I know I can't believe I'm saying it either, but it's true. Was it also just coincidence that the duty padre who performed the last rights on the 50th anniversary of their wedding, was from the same parish and church where my mum and dad got married all those years ago. The very same church where over 33 years previously as a fourteen year old boy I stood there at my dad's funeral. Some things happen for a reason and the turn of events over the next few days where truly unbelievable.

Chapter 6

Bourne Identity

I left the hospital at about 5.30am, took the short drive home, my mind was now racing, I had been given the booklet, *"Dealing with Bereavement"* and was thinking through the list of things to do. Although my mum had remarried both my sister and I agreed that it was better if we took the burden off my stepfather and deal with all the arrangement you are faced with when you lose a loved one. Naturally I did not sleep when I arrived home, Linda was waiting for me and gave me a big hug of reassurance, I said "I'm not going to bed love, just leave me down here for a while I'll be OK". I did manage to get a few hours' sleep but at 9.00am I rushed to have a quick wash and shave, put on my suit and jumped in the car to go to church. I don't even think I said anything to Linda. I drove to St Anne's and was there for the 11 O'clock mass. I just felt that it was something I had to do. Although feeling a little hypocritical as I had not been in that church for a service since my dad died.

As I approached the church I was a little apprehensive, it was like going back in time, growing up as catholic kids we were never out of the place, and it hadn't changed. I sat quietly at the back, the church still looked the same after all these years. I remember seeing the Stations of the Cross, all carved in wood, they still hung on the walls of the church as they had always done. I knelt down and joined in the service, I found myself saying all the responses during the mass despite not having gone to a catholic mass for a very, very long time. I went to receive Holy Communion and saw that the priest giving the service was Father Derrick. After the service I lit four candles, one for my mum, one for my dad and two for my uncles Mark and Tom. I then went to the vestry to see Father Derrick. I told him how special it would be if we could hold the funeral here for my mum, I told him that although we were no longer members of his parish, we had all been brought up in the area and went to St Anne's school when we were kids. Naturally he agreed.

On Monday both my sister and I went to collect the death certificate and then on to the registrar to register the death of our mum. We then went on to the funeral directors to arrange for her body to be removed from the hospital to the chapel of rest. Everything seemed to be happening so quick. It's not that we were in a rush to get her buried we just wanted her out of hospital, she had spent too long in there over the years and we knew how much she hated being in there. (*Although we also knew that she had left that place the second she passed away*).

The problem we were now faced with was that mum had always told us that she wanted to be buried with our dad, not that she didn't love Gerald she did, but this was something she often mentioned to us when we were alone and looking through the old photographs which she kept in her room. Her relationship with Gerald had gone a little cold during the latter years as they were now sleeping in separate rooms. So we both knew that this would cause problems with other members of our extended family, understandably we were faced with a little dilemma.

After visiting the funeral directors Sharon suggested we go to the cemetery and visit dads' grave. I had never actually been to my dad's grave since that day I stood there as a fourteen year old boy. I had a rough idea where the plot was but never really knew where the actual graveside was. My wife reminded me that we did go once, but I wasn't sure if we were standing in the right spot, as we never placed a headstone there. I felt so ashamed, that I had never been back to pay my respects. We drove through the cemetery gates to the area where the plot was.

Sharon told me that she and my mum went there quite often, and a number of years ago planted two small conifers at the head of the plot. I parked the car close by as she pointed out where it was. The two conifers where now so prominent you couldn't have asked for a better marker. I had mixed feelings as we took the short walk to the graveside. Until this point I had not yet shed a tear for my mum and thought that this would be the moment… In addition to the conifers was a small old black graveside pot with the word John painted by hand in yellow paint. I stood in the exact same spot where as a fourteen year old boy I looked down to see my dad's name engraved on the plate of the coffin. Once again there was nothing, no feelings of sadness, no tears, just an immense feeling of guilt, and a voice inside my head saying *"you didn't cry last time you little sod so why cry now, stay strong for your sister"*. We both stood there in silence for a while, until Sharon said *"do you know where granddad Mooney's grave is?"* Obviously not, as up until that point I never even knew where my dad's grave was let alone any other family members. She pointed out a white gravestone about 50 feet away, as I walked towards it I felt a cold shudder down my spine, the first thing I noticed as I got closer was that this was a Military Gravestone. Then as I approached the front of the grave I saw the crest and the name on the headstone. I was frozen to the spot. It was as if time had stopped for a brief moment, while all the images of my life where being played out before me. All the who's, what's and why fore's, like in one of those films when the central character suddenly remembers everything, as his whole life is played out before him. I call this my Jason Bourne moment.

The crest on the headstone was the Fleur-de-lys, of the Manchester Regiment. The Name engraved on the headstone was George Mooney, my dad's elder brother who was killed in action in the Second World War at the age of 33. Sharon told me that George and my dad's other brother Bill and Granddad Mooney where all laid to rest in that plot. As a former soldier I was even more ashamed that I had not known about this grave and its whereabouts.

I was suddenly seven years old again, as I remembered the time of my first communion and the time of receiving the sacrament of confirmation. A time when as a young catholic boy you get to choose another name, traditionally a name of a patron saint. I remember at the time that the name I wanted and eventually chose was George, mainly because of George Best, he was almost every young boys hero growing up in the late 60's, one of the greatest Man United players that ever lived, to many United fans he was indeed St George. All I recall at the time was that my dad said that's a good choice. I didn't even know I had an Uncle George until the moment I saw it on that gravestone. We had lots of aunties and uncles when we were kids, there was actually thirteen children in my dad's family, and my dad was the youngest. The next flash of images and thoughts were when I served with the TA as a Permanent staff Instructor (PSI). Linda and I moved to a married quarter on the outskirts of Ashton under Lyne, every day we drove past the old barracks on Mossley Road which was the home of the Manchester Regiment, this was now a private housing estate, Linda always said that it would be nice to live there, and in 1991 we bought a house at plot number 33, the old barrack wall still surrounds the estate and the original entrance is still standing, a memorial in its own right. With the crest/Fleur-de-lys prominently carved into the arch of the entrance, the very same crest engraved on the Gravestone. Was this just a strong coincidence or was there more to this connection with St George, and the home where we now live. Shortly after moving there I once bought a random picture on Ashton market of soldiers standing outside the Barrack entrance, it still hangs in my office today. One of the reasons I chose this picture was due to the fact that one of the soldiers pictured in it, looks like me, standing in exactly the same way I do in most of my pictures, could this be my uncle George?

When my dad died I often wondered why I joined the army as this seemed to be on a whim, just a knee jerk reaction after leaving school. My dad was a former Navy man, and was still serving when both Mick and I were born. Mick was born in Londonderry while my dad was serving at

Ebrington Barracks. I was born two years later in Glasgow when he was posted to the Naval Base on the Clyde, just before he completed his 12 years' service. So if I was going to join any of the armed service why did I not join the Navy?

I left school in May 1976. A few weeks later I found myself standing outside the Army careers office one day, and simply walked in. I remember seeing pictures of guys jumping out of helicopters and decided that was something I wanted to do. I didn't have a clue what regiment I was joining. When I passed my training as a boy soldier I joined The First Battalion the Royal Regiment of Fusilier. A regiment like many of the former county regiments at the time, one that had three battalions. In normal circumstances I should have joined the 3rd Battalion, as this was the one ordinarily associated with Lancashire, and closely linked to what was once the Lancashire Fusiliers. When the Royal Regiment of Fusiliers were amalgamated on the 23rd April 1969 (St Georges Day), from the former county Regiments of The Northumberland, Lancashire, Royal Fusiliers and Warwickshire Fusiliers, a new recruit from Oldham should have joined the 3rd Battalion as they were predominantly made up of the soldiers from Lancashire and Royal Fusiliers from London. While the first battalion was formed primarily from what was once the Northumberland Fusiliers'. So by now it's likely you are wondering what's the significance to all this?

When I returned home on my very first period of leave, my proud mum asked me to wear my uniform and took my photo in the backyard while standing in front of the back gate, she told me that her brother had served as a Northumberland Fusilier. I always thought that she had her wires crossed, her family roots were all Cheshire related, so why would her brother be drafted to the Northumberland Fusiliers, I always thought that she got it wrong. This was until many years later when we attended my Aunty Mary's funeral. She was my mums' younger sister who lived in Warrington, and sadly died less than two years before my mum. After the funeral while we were sat at my cousins house he gave my mum a small plastic folder that Aunty Mary wanted her to have. It contained photos of Jerry, the brother she had not seen for over 50 years, the brother who she had said served in the Northumberland Fusiliers and moved to South Africa in the early 60's. Sadly he had also died. As my cousin handed her a small clear plastic wallet, I saw that it contained the distinctive Red and White Hackle of the Fusiliers, and a number of pictures, one that was completely unbelievable, he was standing at the back gate in his uniform, my mum said she remembered taking that picture. *Was all this all part of my 'Born Identity'?

*Sorry this is another film reference, and a play on the film title, Bourne Identity, where the central character Jason Bourne loses his memory. There is a scene in the movie where he starts to recall his true identity, hence the significance to the title of this particular chapter.

All these thoughts came flooding back to me while I was standing by this Military graveside. Perhaps I was just making it all fit; nonetheless it was such a strange and vivid experience to be simply coincidence. Why were all these images suddenly being shown to me, it was as if I was piecing together my life, like a scene from my very own, "Who do you think you are?" TV show, it was truly unbelievable. When we are born we inherit genes from our parents, but what do we inherit spiritually from other members of the family. I can understand that at a time of grief our minds are more open to suggestion, but all this was just too weird, or was I simply going crazy.

My mums funeral went ahead as planned, the service was held at St Anne's Church and Father Derrick delivered a requiem mass, mum was buried just a few feet away from my dad's grave. We decided against burying her with dad, despite what she had said, my mum was a good one for keeping the peace, she was after all Gerald's wife now, and although they had their up's and downs they still loved each other very much.

A few weeks after the funeral my business started to take a downward spiral. I completely lost the momentum. Was I using my mums passing as an excuse for my own failings...? Or was this the result of grief, once again I held on to all my emotions, I simply bottled everything up, not allowing anyone in, to what was going on inside my head.

Chapter 7

Procrastination

The Death of a Business

Things went from bad to worse with the business. I was paying out more in late penalty fees for not completing returns on time, and some for not submitting them at all. The cost of putting things off was now starting to hurt me. I was now also falling behind on my mortgage.

Despite all this I still had a belief that I could make it in the business world. What I failed to see was how this was affecting my family, mainly my wife Linda, who said very little, as always she continued to let me just get on with it. She had faith in what I was doing.

We often go through life totally blinkered and fail to see what is happening around us. Linda also had her own problems to deal with and often immersed herself in her own families' troubles. Although she was not the oldest member of her family of four brothers and two sisters, she seemed to take on-board everyone else's trials and tribulation. Linda was always the one her sisters turned to when they had problems, she was and still is a true listener, a quality that's needed in all relationships. Something I wish I was better at.

One particular quest or should I say crusade, she embarked on, as this gives it more meaning based on the Oxford English Dictionary's definition *"a long and determined attempt to achieve something that you believe in strongly"*. This was the support and commitment she showed for her eldest brother, who at the time was totally drink dependant. Once a proud man and one we all looked up to when we were kids. Sadly he was a man who became a victim of loneliness depression and alcohol addiction. I'd been with Linda since the age of fifteen and witnessed myself the effects drink had on him, it was sad to see this happening.

Linda and her younger sister took on a huge personal challenge and a promise to their mum that they would fix this problem. Linda's mum sadly died before this transformation took place, but together they did it, through relentless perseverance, love and support.

Prior to this miraculous recovery Brian had spent a good few months in hospital after he fell and broke his hip. This was just before Christmas 2008 and only a few weeks after Linda's mum died. As a result of the fall he was admitted to hospital. They later found that he had suffered a mini stoke, undoubtedly brought on by his drinking. The immediate treatment he received was shocking to say the least, especially when he was admitted, however they would not let the hospital give up on him. Most people in his condition are given far less sympathy and attention, in some hospitals alcoholics appear to be treated differently; perhaps it's not seen as an illness or a disease. It's as if they don't see the person behind this condition. Maybe they just see a faceless drunk with a self-inflicted dependency. But he was their big brother nothing was going to stop them and they never gave up or let people put things off, especially were his treatment was a concern. Christmas came and went so did spring, it was a relentless effort and they got the results they wanted. He was finally discharged, and in much better health than he was. Although now a recovering alcoholic he continues to get their love and support week after week. They will never give up on him.

Closer to home we still had our own problems when in June 2009 I eventually received a winding up order due to the fact that I could not pay a £15,000 debt accrued, this time in Corporation Tax, (*oh the joys of owning and running a Limited Company eh*), in truth I probably didn't even owe that much. If I had only been as relentless as my wife had been in her quest to help her brother, unfortunately my procrastination had finally come to fruition and I was now in deep shit, there was no other way to describe it. In addition to this we also received a court order on our mortgage; they were going to take our house away. It was time for me to pull my socks up, this was a big wakeup call; although it did come down to us going to court, but there was no way I was going to lose my house. Even if it meant that I would have to pay a higher mortgage fee to pay off the arrears.

So I went back to basics, although the Limited Company was wound up, I could still work under my own name. I could still make money on the internet as an affiliate; the directory domain names were still mine, as this was something I owned before I created a limited company. As a result I was able to pay off some of the mortgage arrears and save our home, but this was a continuous upward struggle.

I could of course declared myself bankrupt, but that was not something I was going to do, for me bankruptcy meant total failure. Then came the next bombshell…

While driving home from a regular visit to Linda's brother, on a dark foggy night in November that same year, on a route home we had taken many times before. Linda just let out a scream "STOP THE CAR STOP THE CAR"! I thought she was having a heart attack or something; she was just shaking with fear. I had never witnessed someone having a panic attack before. Her breathing was erratic; all the colour had drained from her face. I said I'll take you to hospital which was less than a mile from our house, but she said no just take me home, I want to go home, take me home. She seemed to calm down when we got in the house; she just sat there in silence. Little did I know that there was something more serious going on?

It was as if all the strength had been drained out of her, everything she had coped with over the last few years, and all the uncertainty I had put her through, plus the loss of her mum, the support for her brother, and the possibility of losing her home. It had all finally taken its toll on this fantastic woman. It was weeks before she would eventually leave the house, only then would she walk to the end of our road just a few metres, and only if I was with her. She was even frightened of having a bath, she would only fill it just an inch or two. Her weight dropped dramatically, she wasn't eating properly it was a very difficult and worrying time for both of us. She was also unable to go to work which no doubt added to our financial burden.

During this time I still had the problem of TAX bills and just three weeks before Christmas I received a call from a TAX inspector, I had not submitted a self-assessment tax return for the previous year, so they simply decided to asses this based on previous earnings, it wasn't that I hadn't received any letters or reminders, I had, but chose to ignore them.

I was now faced with a Tax Inspector standing on the doorstep to collect the money, a debt to the crown, my time was up. If you have ever been visited by the tax man you will know that you can't just say the cheque is in the post. They want their pound of flesh, and he wanted £3000, pounds. I managed to convince him that I would pay this sum before Christmas, I felt a little guilty using bereavement as an excuse, nonetheless he agreed but not without me signing a Distraint Order for my car. I was about to have one of the worst Christmases of my life. All the money I was now making was being handed over to bailiffs and on Christmas Eve when I drove to their offices in Salford to hand over £1500 in cash, my final payment on this particular tax bill, I felt totally defeated. I was once again the Best Loser, simply fighting hard and getting nowhere. The funny thing was the car was only worth five or six hundred pounds, but I would have been lost without it.

At times during that particular Christmas and New Year I felt like giving up completely. My beautiful wife was a shell of her former self, if it wasn't for her I would have done something stupid.

Was this another test? Was this one of those self-inflicted life experiences we subject ourselves to, but feel that it's everyone else's fault? I had read a number of books on tackling procrastination, but still found it hard to focus. Procrastination was my vice; it was my disease, my addiction, eating away at me like my very own cancer. I always found something better to do, instead of doing the important stuff. Perhaps writing this book will be part of that cure, will I ever finish something without being distracted? If you are reading this you will already know that I have come a long way to finding my own cure.

What is procrastination anyway? I had read the book "Eat That Frog" by Brian Tracy, plus many more. But as far as I was concerned it's not just about putting things off and doing the less important or more enjoyable stuff, was it that I enjoyed putting myself under pressure? Was I leaving things to the last minute simply to feel the strain of the pending consequence it resulted in? On more than one of my military reports is would often say "works well under pressure". Was it simply pressure I was looking for? Perhaps there was something else. In many books on the subject they also say that procrastination is something we all suffer from at times in our lives, perhaps some more than others. It's also believed to be closely linked to depression. All I know at the time of writing this particular chapter is that procrastination killed my business. Not only that, it also affected others. I needed to find a solution.

Although the purpose of this book isn't to simply highlight the effects, symptoms or cures for procrastination, I want it to be more than that. I have learnt that the first step with any form of addiction is admitting you have a problem and eventually realising the serious implications it can have, not only on you but the ones you love; this for me is the first step to curing this disease. Unfortunately there were more dark days ahead before I finally decided to tackle this problem head on.

It seems ironic that this is one of the shortest chapters in the book, perhaps it's just that I want to move on to the next chapter so I can finally finish something I have started.

Chapter 8

More Dark Days Ahead

2010 was going to be my year; I had planned to go on a cruise with Linda, a birthday treat I was going to give myself for surviving 50 years on this planet. I'd not really celebrated any of my significant birthdays. Being born in mid-January had its downside over the years, as there never seemed to be any money left in the pot for my birthday, sounds selfish, I know.

My first memory of this was when I was seven years old, another one of those life experiences etched in my mind forever, although we never expected much in those days, my mum would always do her best to provide us with something. Unfortunately on that day mum was in hospital having gallstones removed. I remember going to see her in the afternoon and although it wasn't much to shout about these days, she gave me a bar of Cadburys Fruit & Nut, having a whole bar to yourself was a real treat back in 1967. My dad also said that he had made me a cake which we're going to have for tea when we got home.

I had never had a birthday cake before and was excited to see what he had made for me. When mum was in hospital or it was his turn to make the tea, which wasn't that often, he did however make the best cheese and onion pies I have ever tasted, which he made on individual saucers. After our tea we all sat in the front room with the lights off waiting for the cake. I could hear him striking matches in the kitchen, then the sound of "Happy Birthday to you... Happy

Birthday to you..." as he walked in I could hear our Mick laughing, I turned around to see that he was carrying a large spud on a plate with seven matches in... No cake, there was no cake, everyone was laughing, not me, this wasn't a prank where the cake then appears when the joke wears off.

This was not funny, because all the way home from the hospital I was thinking about my cake, to a seven year old this was a cruel trick. A memory I never forgot, but it prepared me for all those years to come, no other birthday was ever as disappointing as that one. I grew up never expecting much for my birthday, like many families growing up in the late 60's and early 70's we never had much anyway. To be honest we never expected much, there was a saying my mum would often say "you get what you are given". If you asked, what's for tea mum? She would always reply "shit with sugar on". To be honest her food was quite good.

At thirteen I got my first real bike, not as a birthday or Christmas present it was one I bought myself for £2.50 from a second hand shop on Huddersfield Road. I remember it being a long walk to this particular shop. It also took me two weeks to pay for it from the money I saved from my Paper round. To find a bike in a second hand shop was actually quite rare, unlike today were you see one on every street corner and every High Street, bikes are in abundance at the many Cash Converter outlets.

I was never off that bike. A bike to a young lad then seemed so special, it gave you freedom, a chance to escape, either alone or with a small group of mates. Back then we were all mad on cycle speedway, we created our own track at the back of our house on a waste piece of ground we called the croft.

Our bikes were all practically homemade by the time we had finished modifying them. The main characteristics would be that they had no brakes, as this was a key feature to a real Speedway Bike, *(The motorized version, used by our heroes at Bell Vue Aces)*, as they were simply controlled by the clutch and also had no brakes. Stopping our bikes was actually quite a skill, you had to lean right over to the left or right, take your foot off the pedal and perform a skid which we called a broadside. If you have ever seen the kids in the Film ET in the final bike chase scene, you can see them doing it. The other key feature is that our bikes had to have straight forks, as this gives you more pull on the front wheel. For those of you who remember the bikes that I grew up with they all had curved forks, apart from the famous 1970's CHOPPER, almost all bikes today have straight forks.

To straighten our forks we would simply take off the front wheel, rest the forks on the kerb, with the curve side uppermost, we would then proceed to bash the crap out of them with a full house brick until they were straight. *(We were true pioneers of the modern BMX and mountain bike)*. One other main component was that we had to have one large fixed gear. Back then if you had brakes and gears on your bike you were a poof, *(although we didn't quite know what a poof was)*. The large fixed gear meant that you could accelerate quickly at the start of the race, and as you come out of a bend, the equivalent to being in first gear on today's modern bikes. Each race would be four laps of the track, we would spend all day doing this come rain or shine, in between fixing the punctures and applying sticking plasters and Germolene® to our knees, arms and elbows when we fell off at speed. Gravel rash was an occupational hazard.

Our backyard was the nearest to the croft and quite often became the pit stop, the amount of bent spoons you could find in my mums kitchen drawer was like a visit from a Uri Geller convention. Why I never grew up to be a mechanic I will never know, I really did love that bike.

As the years past I never seemed to get anything special for my birthdays, nothing I can remember. Therefore over the years there was a trend developing, serving in the armed forces had its disadvantages and most of my birthdays were spent away, especially the important one's 21st, 30th, 40th, all spent away from home, either on operations somewhere in the world, sat in a trench watching it fill with water or standing on a cordon in Northern Ireland, no party, no celebration, and no fecking cake.

So this 50 years celebration was going to be the BIG one. I was in control… well I thought I was. Little did I know that my wife would at the time be suffering from GAD, General Anxiety Disorder? It's actually more serious than it sounds, and now being unable to leave the house, getting on a boat was out of the question. In addition to this, as I said the Taxman came knocking. My trip of a lifetime would have to wait, so this was another one of those disappointments, I was seven years old again, simply left feeling sorry for myself.

I did my best to soldier on and immersed myself in my training for the London and Edinburgh Marathons, in April and May that year… Another goal I had set myself for my 50th year. I was going to be FAST at 50 (Fit and Still Training at 50). Ironically yet another website I set up for myself, I even went as far as having tee-shirts printed, another distraction from what was going on around me at the time.

Running a marathon is a great metaphor for what life often throws at you. Sometimes you find yourself running with the pack, some get to the finish before you, the majority are on a personal journey, but all heading in the same direction, and that last 3 miles is also a real test of mental strength. For those who have achieved and experienced this will know what I mean.

For me running has always been my way of escaping, clearing my head, fixing the problems of the day, working out solutions, as crazy as it sounds I also like the challenge of blocking out the pains in my knees, by focusing my mind on other thoughts. I'm not a particularly fast runner, but can still maintain an average 8 minute mile, sometimes seven on a good day, over the distance of 13 .2 miles, the second half of the marathon was a little longer, I think my last mile was 15 minutes on the day of the London Marathon. At the 22 mile point I wanted to walk, the pain in my upper thighs was indescribable, for me walking was not an option. My official time was 4hrs 46min 12sec. Not my best time but I suppose still not too shabby for a 50 year old, with arthritic knees.

Looking back the training was a perfect distraction for what was going on around me. When I first left the Army over 10 years ago I visualised that by this time I would be well on my way to being a successful businessman, instead I was still in debt, still struggling to pay creditors, all the pressure was now beginning to take its toll. I was starting to experience failure.

Although my body was fit and healthy the things going on inside my head were not. I had witnessed first-hand what depression can do to you. My wife was still not 100% although she had started working again, and the tablets she was prescribed seemed to help, I was worried that she was becoming addicted. I felt totally responsible.

I remember thinking about how well my younger brother and sister had done for themselves. My sister in particular who rescued herself from a broken marriage. Through sheer hard work and determination, she was now in a happy relationship and about to re-marry. My younger brother also seemed to have everything he wanted. He had left the Army five years after me, had a beautiful home, a second home in France and was also getting married for the second time. Although my older brother had suffered a major brain injury and was in a residential care home, I imagined that he had no worries, he seemed quite content in his own little world. That may sound a little shallow, but those were the thoughts I was having at this time.

In part I was proud of what my younger siblings had achieved, but jealous at the same time. The only thing I knew I got right first time was that I married the right girl.

What I started to doubt more than anything were my own abilities, what was I working for? Was all this pressure I was putting myself under really worth it?

I looked around at the possessions we had, understandably there are many who would give their right arm for a fraction of what I had, but we never see it like that. There might be that brief moment while watching programmes like Children in Need or Comic Relief, when we are reminded of how lucky we are, but that moment never seems to last. All it takes is that bill to land on the doorstep or that thought of self-doubt to enter your head and bang! You are back to feeling sorry for yourself, I needed a way out.

I don't really remember that much of 2011, only that I was treading water, simply going nowhere just about keeping my head above the water line. Still self-employed, just making enough money to keep the house going. I ran an online course for a while for would-be Internet Marketers, teaching them how to make money online, building websites and creating web content that generated an income. At times I felt a little hypocritical, although I was making some money, and not just from what they were paying me, the truth is, I had lost the passion for it. When I spoke to some of them on Skype I knew that they had probably paid me money they couldn't quite afford. It's easy to take money off desperate people and there are lots of people getting rich off the backs of those following a dream. Just look in the self-help section in any book shop, Books by Jack Canfield, Tony Robbins, Paul McKenna, to name but a few, all these guys have made millions selling these books on the topic of self-help/motivation. I too have bought most of them or listened to audio versions. These books are all good at giving you that quick injection of inspiration or motivation. Eventually you realise that reading the book is not the answer, more on that later.

In 2011 I simply lost the plot. I had spent just over ten years in what I call the Civvy Street Maze and I was totally disorientated. My emotions and feelings seemed all over the place. In the Army you had a system, direction; you could see progress developing in front of you. You learned how to use your inner compass. If you were ambitious it was easy to see how much progress you were making. Life was different in the realm of Civvy Street. Progress/success appeared to be measured by wealth and possessions; if that was truly the case I was failing badly.

During this dark time in my life on many occasions I would simply sit in my office stirring at the computer screen, occasionally checking my accounts on the various Affiliate Marketing Networks to see how much money I had made, or not in most cases. I spent whole days simply doing nothing. I would pace up and down, walk outside, start something, than just stop and start something else. Working from home is quite often a lonely existence, especially when you feel unproductive. If all else failed I would simply go for a run.

The problem now being were just a few months ago running was a way to find inspiration, now all my thoughts were about failure/negative emotions, the run would turn into a walk, as I would often give up as I let the pain in my knees beat me. I thought to myself... at this time just less than a year ago I had ran in two major marathons, completed the Great North Run with over 40.000 runners. Running was exciting, a challenge, what was happening to me?

One day I stopped sat down by a large tree, looked up at the branches and thought... FUCK IT! ... I started to remove the draw cord from my tracksuit bottoms. I had these thoughts before but this time I was going to do it. I am not sure what stopped me climbing that tree that day, but I came very close to the inevitable outcome.

It is often said that this is a coward's way out, but no one really knows what goes on inside the head of someone about to commit suicide. Well not the successful ones, it's all so easy to pass judgement, I know I have in the past. Personally I had clearly had enough; but not quite sure what stopped me? Perhaps it was the thought that this wasn't right, something I remember from my childhood, being brought up in a Catholic School. We were told as kids that killing yourself was a mortal sin and we would go to hell. I'm not quite sure if this is what stopped me, or was it that I would bring shame on my family. I suppose those that succeed simply blank out all emotion, or perhaps part of the brain that controls rational thought simply closes down. All I remember from that day is that for some reason I simply decided to stand up and walk away.

During my time in the Army three people I knew quite well all ended their own lives; two hung themselves and one shot himself with an air rifle. They all received military funerals with full military honours. Many of my former colleagues questioned this, why should they... they took the cowards way out? I attended all their funerals and remember seeing the faces of the immediate family, in particular the faces of two young boys, one guy in particular left without a dad. Perhaps I subconsciously revisited these images in my mind.

One particular funeral was that of the young guy who shot himself. When we heard that he did it with an air rifle, we all immediately thought how the hell can you kill yourself with an air rifle? He actually shot himself through the eye socket and the pellet penetrated his brain and caused internal bleeding, he subsequently died of a brain haemorrhage.

On this particular occasion I was appointed as the Funeral Party Sergeant Major, my job was to oversee the whole proceedings of the military funeral, this was one of the most challenging appointments you are called upon to take, but one I had done before. The whole funeral parade is your total responsibility, all eyes are on you. The first time I had the honour of conducting this parade was for one of our soldiers who sadly died of leukaemia at the age of 28. It's actually quite an honour to oversee such an important event. The second time I was serving as a Senior Permanent Staff Instructor (SPSI), with the Territorial Army. This was the young guy who killed himself he was a TA soldier, none of us knew why he decided to end his own life in such a way. He came from a privileged background, his father was a professor at one of the local universities, the guys who knew him quite well just couldn't understand why he did this.

My biggest fear at the time was that I had to get these guys from the TA to perform some of the trickiest drill movements in the book. Getting some of them just to march in a straight line was a tall order for any sergeant major. The average TA Soldier is not renowned for his drill and bearing, some are not considered the smartest, *(in the dress sense that is)*, so I had my work cut out. Nonetheless after much practice they did not let me down. Although we did nickname one guy *Victor Meldrew, after he fell in a grave during a practice run through.

So was it these images/memories that stopped me that day. Looking back now I know there were many more occasions when ending my life was almost a daily occurrence. Although at times it was primarily money worries that triggered off most of these negative thoughts, a sense of being a failure or quite simply the Best Loser, was a thought that seemed to stay with me.

During the final quarter of 2011 I was at my lowest yet, not having enough money to get my car through its MOT was one contributing factor. Understandably some people would give their right arm just to own a car, but once you lose something you rely on, it soon starts to affect you. At the end of each day I would take the three mile walk to meet my wife from work.

If you don't know the significance of reference to Victor Meldrew, he was a character in a 1990's sitcom "On Foot in the Grave".

I would much rather walk than get a bus to town. We would then both take the long walk home, it always seemed longer as we walked uphill. I called this *"the walk of shame"*. Especially when walking with two bags of food we bought from the money we saved by not getting the bus. With my head down and the handles of the bags cutting off the blood supply to my fingers I would reflect on how it had all come to this.

On those trips home there were times when we never spoke. I just kept my head down hoping that none of the neighbours would drive past and see us on our walk of shame, carrying our ICELAND bags while they were on their way to Sainsbury's. (*I know quite shallow*).

As we approached November things were getting worse, my car was still sat on the drive untaxed, no MOT, although it was still insured. The thought of torching it did enter my head but I am sure the insurance company would work out my not so devious claim. The continuous walk of shame now meant that I had holes in my shoes, which only added to my self-pity. I know there were people worse off than me, but when you lose your pride and self-esteem no one else matters.

I did my best to try and pick myself up and think happy thoughts, I even booked myself in at the Comedy Store in Manchester, taking part in the King Gong Competition. You only have to last five minutes on stage for a chance of winning £50.00. It was free to enter and you get a free drink. So I dusted off my old dinner jacket and black tie, polished my old George Boots I still had in the cupboard, as these were the only things without holes in.

The only routine I could remember was an old chicken gag I had performed many times before. As I arrived I quickly realised that I was the oldest in the place, as it was full of students on a cheap night out. This was a tough crowd, the competition is quite simple, you just have to last five minutes on stage beating the Gong! Three members of the audience are given cards to hold up if they think you are rubbish, if all three cards are up then you are off... I knew it was going to be tough when the first guy only lasted about 5 seconds. When my turn came I actually felt quite comfortable, I told myself that I was not going to swear, but after seeing all the other acts, swearing was considered quite normal.

I didn't win but did manage to reach the punch line of my gag lasting just under five minutes. The problem for me was that this was another defeat, something else to beat myself up about. You often hear that many comedians are manic depressives and performing comedy is part of the escape. Although I wouldn't quite rank myself as a comedian I had actually displayed one of the major symptoms' of depression.

About a week later I walked into the doctor's surgery to book an appointment for my knee. This was an ongoing problem I had as a result of all the previous running. When I got to see my doctor after the obligatory wait of three or four weeks, OK a slight exaggeration, it was a few days. I sat in his surgery and he asked me what's wrong. I felt like an alcoholic admitting for the first time to their addiction.

As I looked at him I could feel my eyes simply filling with tears as they started to roll down my face. Wiping them away I just broke down and said I think I'm suffering from depression. I remember him asking me lots of questions, after which he gave me a prescription for Citalopram, apparently the prescribed drug common for people with depression and anxiety. Apparently they work by increasing levels of serotonin in the brain.

Understandably things did not improve immediately in fact they seemed to get worse, we were now approaching December Christmas was on the horizon, plus my Stepdad was admitted to hospital with stomach cancer, something we didn't actually find out about until late January. Money was tighter than ever and the day I walked to Cash Converters to pawn my beloved saxophone was a day I admitted defeat. I had all intentions of buying it back just a few weeks later so only asked for £130.00, it was worth much more.

Although I was never a true master of the sax it did remind me of a time when things weren't quite so bad. One of my fondest memories was during a family get together, when we all sat around at my sister in laws house on New Year's Eve and we played name that tune for chicken drumsticks, and then went out into the street to play Auld Lang Sine. The way I played the saxophone was similar to the way Les Dawson played the piano, like him I hit the bum notes deliberately, (well that's what I told people). My sister in law moved house not long after that, I wonder why?

Another memorable time was when I took it on a Night Noise Demo, while serving with the Officer Training Corps on Otterburn Training Area in Northumberland. Our Commanding Officer at the time was a bit of a traditionalist, a cavalry officer who wasn't that familiar with the sense of humour of a Northern RSM. The night noise demo was a fieldcraft exercise were soldiers or in this case young officer cadets would sit on a hillside late at night and listen to various noises to identify the sound and approximate location and direction of the noise using a compass bearing. Little did they expect the RSM to be stood on a hill over 1000 metres away playing the theme tune to the Pink Panther, loud and proud at midnight. It was one of those, you had to be there moments to appreciate it. It's funny I would often say to the kids that if you ever see me sat outside Mc Donald's with my sax and a hat at my feet, then you know things aren't too great.

So walking into Cash Converters was a real blow for me, pardon the pun. The £130.00 was used to buy Christmas presents for the kids. I had all intentions of buying it back in January as Birthday present to myself, but like all my birthdays I was disappointed once again and never really had the money to get it back.

In January my stepdad was diagnosed with cancer and we were faced with another family crisis. This was perhaps my wake up call. It was time to get a grip!

Chapter 9

Quit to Succeed

In many of the self-help books I had read, there was one phrase I came across quite often. *"Sometimes you simply have to quit to succeed"*. Quit what? The problem many of us face is knowing what it is we must quit.

Although it was not in my nature to give up on anything I realised that I needed to simply say no to depression. The tablets I was prescribed were in some way adding to my feeling of defeat, simply by taking them I felt that I had given in to depression. At this time my wife was still taking her daily dose and seemed totally dependent on them. Although they may have helped me in some small way, after a month of taking them they were starting to take effect, in more ways than one, as with all prescribed drugs they do have side effects. I didn't want to become totally reliant on them. I remember religiously having to take my wife to the doctors to get that new prescription as it was one date we could never miss. So it was now my turn. I took my last tablet from the blister packet popped in my mouth, swallowed and walked down to the doctor's surgery for my next fix.

I watched as he typed into the computer the details of my next prescription. I remember the days when all this stuff was handwritten. You could never read a prescription back them. He handed it to me. I could see that he had prescribed a course of another 56 days of Citalopram 20mg tablets. It was dated the 19th January 2012, just one day after my 52nd birthday. I stood outside the chemist with my new prescription in my hand, knowing that I needed £7.50 to pay for the tablets. I'm not quite sure why but I simply walked away, perhaps it was the fact that £7.50 would be far better spent on something for tea that night, than a course of happy pills. I took the walk of shame home with just one thought inside my head. I had said no to depression. My head was once again racing with the thought that we must first quit to succeed. That walk home seemed longer than ever, I thought about all the things I needed to do, what was it that was holding me back and why was it that I never seemed to move forward.

When I got home I went and sat in my office, my Tax Return was on the desk still not filled out. I pinned the prescription to my notice board just in case I changed my mind. I looked down at the unfinished Tax Return, the deadline was just a few days away. It was then when I realised what it was I need to quit to succeed. Although being self-employed had its benefits, the financial mess I had got myself in was no doubt a result of self-employment. Within a few hours I had completed my Tax Return, which was a first for me. I normally leave it to the very last minute or wait for the charges to mount up before completing it. I took the short walk to the post box and mailed it. I remember thinking at the time I don't want to do this anymore.

There were times while serving in the army when people I knew in Civvy Street would often say it's alright for you, everything is done for you, at the time I would always disagree and defend my corner. Now I fully understood what they meant. In the army I never had to worry about money, it was always in the bank at the end of the month, if I was ill I never had to wait more than a few hours to see a doctor. I never paid for prescriptions, or gym fees, never filled a Tax return or had to pay Corporation Tax, whatever it was I needed was right there in front of me. Its funny how we take things for granted but still find time to complain.

That afternoon I dusted off my old CV and thought long and hard about what it was I really wanted to do, it was time to start job hunting. I reminded myself of the things I enjoyed most over the years, teaching, training, and influencing others. It was at that point when I remembered seeing something in the local paper about Military Mentors working in Free Schools, were ex-service personnel were involved in teaching kids who had lost their way, kids who had been excluded from main stream education. I switched on the computer and searched the internet and found links to a website called Skill Force. I discovered that this was a charity set up by one of my old Company Commanders. I submitted the online application, and within a few days I got a call to go and visit the team that worked in Manchester. The office they worked from at the time was located in a large mill in Failsworth. I met with this young woman who gave me much more of an insight into what they did and that they were looking primarily for part time tutors. The only problem I faced was that I needed to have a PTTLS qualification a minimum of level 3 as this was a requirement for their funding. Unfortunately this was one qualification I did not have at the time. PTTLS *(Preparing to Teach in The*

Lifelong Learning Sector) is a City and Guilds qualification, which is considered the first step towards teaching in post-compulsory education. Although this was something I completed later at Level 4, at the time of the interview I did not have the money needed to pay for the course. So I never followed up on this opportunity. Although this brief visit did give me a kick up the backside as I knew that I could always find something Part-Time.

Throughout the next few days I continued to search online, submitting my CV to all the employment websites I could find. Routinely checking my inbox for replies which never came, apart from one… I remember watching the postman walk towards the house, I always had mail, normally big brown envelopes from the taxman, the bank, mortgage reminders or other creditors, no offers of jobs or interviews. That prescription pinned on my notice board was looking likely to be cashed in. The depression was starting to take hold once more. Visits to the hospital to see my stepdad were also now a daily occurrence, as his situation was getting worse.

I was desperate to get a reply from someone, at one point I was applying for anything, even pushing trolleys around ASDA car park was one option I thought about. One afternoon I checked my inbox and finally there was a reply. Ironically it was from Royal Mail, the one company that I thought would send replies by post, they didn't in fact they never do as all replies are sent by text or email. To be honest I don't really know why I applied to be a postman, I hated the one we had, not personally. It's just that he always seemed to bring bills and bad news. Perhaps I would get more pleasure from delivering bills than receiving them. But I was pleased that I had at least secured an interview at the Oldham office for a job as a Part Time Postman, not my ideal job choice, but it was an offer, so I attended the interview.

On arrival I met a guy called Nick, one of the senior line managers tasked with overseeing the interview. He seemed to listen intently as I answered his questions. The interview seemed to go OK apart from the fact that my driving licence was showing that I had nine points. The maximum requirement for the job spec was just six. As a matter of fact this was a genuine mistake by the DVLA and I did only have six points and not nine. It was yet another thing I had neglected to sort out when I had the chance, in fact at this particular time the mistake happened over two years ago. I never actually sent my licence back to get the points revoked due to a mistake on their part. It took me almost two weeks to sort it out. I resubmitted my licence some weeks later, taking it personally to the office in Oldham. Although I thought that this was yet another opportunity missed, so didn't think I would hear anything back.

I never applied for any more jobs after that. I just carried on with what little work I had from my website business, and totally forgot about all about Royal Mail. My stepdad was now terminally ill with cancer, so understandably at times my mind was on other things. Although we were never that close he was still the guy who helped my mum keep the family together after my dad died.

The Best Loser

Gerald was a very proud man and at 83 he had never been in hospital or ill, apart for the odd cold or flu. He was also the type of guy who would have a go at anything, most of the time you would find him in the shed or under the car, fixing stuff. The type of guy who would fix stuff even if it wasn't broken. The old saying "if it's not broke why fix it" was more like, ifs it's not broke I will take it apart just so I can fix it, was more a kin to Gerald. At 82 he was still climbing ladders rescuing damsels in distress, as we learned from his next door neighbour who had locked herself out of her house. He got in by climbing though a two story window like some demented OAP cat burglar.

Gerald came into our lives just a year after my dad died, which I found a little too soon for my liking. I can't truly recall how I felt when my mum first introduced me to him back in 1975 at the age of fifteen. I suppose my hormones where all over the place. Initially I saw him as an intruder, so we were never that close. I joined the army not long after so I never became as close to him as my younger sister or brother did. Looking back now, I can see that my mum had made the right move all those years ago. To me he was simply Gerald, but to my sister and younger brother he was a good father figure and later a very much loved granddad to my nieces. Sadly Gerald died in March that year, but not after insisting to the hospital staff that he needed to be at home. Which they eventually agreed to, he died just 20 minutes after being back in his own home. He was certainly a guy who knew his own mind, things were most certainly his was or no way.

Once again we found ourselves organising another family funeral, understandably this was another sad occasion for us all. During this time I started to feel much more tearful than I thought I would. I suppose I realised that Gerald was perhaps a big influence on our family and that he was a significant figure in helping to shape all our futures. One of the saddest moments was clearing the home and belongings both my mum and Gerald shared over the years. Although my mum had died just over four years earlier this was still her home, so it was sad to help clear it of all those memories. Although this was not the house we grew up in, the pictures, ornaments' were all familiar. It's funny how significant something as simple as a bent spoon can help to spark off a memory.

It was during this week I received a text from Royal Mail offering me a job at the Oldham Delivery Office, with a start date of the 3rd of April. I thought that was an opportunity that had passed me by. Although I did give it some thought, did I really want to be a postman? Was quitting the world of self-employment the one thing I needed to do for a while? Perhaps this was the answer, only time will tell.

Chapter 10

From Pillar to Post

On the 3rd of April 2012 I drove to the Royal Mail Sorting and Distribution Offices in Manchester for my induction and the start of what I thought could be a new career with Royal Mail Group Ltd. The induction started with a tour of this large complex and an insight into how mail is delivered throughout the UK and overseas. I listened intently to the guy from the recruiting team as he explained the fundamentals of the Royal Mail infrastructure. He spoke briefly about the internal security operatives and their role, as some kind of clandestine ninja undercover types. Whose job it is to catch out unsuspecting postmen and women who think they can exploit the opportunities of handling sensitive mail, i.e. the valuable stuff. One thought filled my head, *"I could do that job"* the sneaky stuff, not the pilfering, and suddenly the appeal of Royal Mail was becoming more interesting.

The reality was, like all my fellow inductees, we were all just postmen and women, a job that is far from glamorous, which I later found out the following day. That first day was a blur, in less than two hours of entering the building at Oldham we found ourselves out on a delivery, walking through the snow, *yes it did snow in April*, pushing letters through letterboxes. Not the most taxing of jobs, but one that still required some concentration, not just making sure you were posting letters through the right letterboxes, but also avoiding the snow covered dog shit on the pavements of the unsavoury council estate we were delivering on. My previous years as a man in suit and tie had no doubt turned me into a bit of a snob. Although I had been brought up close to some of these areas I now found myself delivering mail to, they were not areas I would normally frequent, (*snobbish comment*). I was having second thoughts about this job even before I was issued the uniform.

Having previously signed a three month contract, I was obliged to continue anyway, so I soldiered on for the first three months. I was now getting better at avoiding the dog shit and as we approached the summer months it seemed to be a much better job when the weather was good.

The contract was only temporary so I still had my sights on other things. The weeks soon become months and before I realised it I was approaching the winter months once again. In just over six months I had lost at least 3 stone in weight. I had cheekbones once again, I felt fitter than I had ever felt for a long time. The tax man was happy as I was finally making regular payments in income tax and national insurance, although there was very little in the way of a wage at the end of it. At times though I often thought what the hell am I doing here especially when it was raining and someone is bending your ear about the price of a first class stamp? Although I had experienced weather and climates far more extreme than the torrential downpours' we were experiencing at the time, to be honest I hated it.

This was also the time when Royal Mail had also just announced that they were increasing the price of First Class Mail to 60p. I remember people being in uproar at such an expense. Understandably there have been times when I would have loved to have 60p in my pocket. But when you are standing on a doorstep, dripping wet, soaked to you bones, with a letter in your hand, that has travelled the length and breadth of the country, and you have personally spent 5 hours walking the streets in the pissing rain, getting it to its final destination. Listening to someone complain that a First Class Stamp costs 60p, you just feel like shouting, "ITS SIXTY FUCKING PENCE LOVE!" you can't even get a bus to Oldham for that price. But you don't you smile nod your head and walk on through the rain.

Although this was a job I hated at times, I do believe that it did in a way save my life. The first year was difficulty, as I know I was still not fully cured of depression, as I often felt quite low at times, but the job did help to keep me busy. Plus I met some interesting people along the way, perhaps this is what I needed, being around other people on a day to day basis. It's well documented that people with depression often lock themselves away, both in their own head and by avoiding contact with others, certainly outside the immediate family.

During the latter part of that first year I found myself working with different people every week, sometimes every day, as I was bounced around from one Walk to another. This was due to the reorganisation of Royal Mail at the time, as many of the new recruits like me were used to fill gaps, while the transition to a fully mobile force was introduced. In outline the old system was changed from postmen and women working independently on a single walk (postal round) to, two posties sharing a van and covering more ground, while also delivering more parcels, which we love apparently, (sorry *private postie joke*).

At first I was a little reluctant to tell my fellow postie colleagues what I did prior to joining Royal Mail, when I did it raised the question I was often asked, "*Why did you give it all up just to be a postman*"? At times I wondered if I had lowered my sights too low, should I be doing something more with the skills I had? I would often lie awake at night thinking, if there was actually a future for me with Royal Mail, was it too late for me? Did I actually want to do anything more than just deliver mail?

While serving in the army I was once in a position to command over 650 people. I once had my own business, a pillar in the community, well sort of. Had I quite literally gone from pillar to post? The thought of being the best loser continued to haunt me. During that first year I hoped that I didn't bump into people I knew while wearing my Royal Mail uniform, for some reason I felt a little embarrassed. The worst times were when I was actually delivering mail to the same houses I once delivered newspapers to as a little kid in short pants. I thought O my god, I'm 52 and was still doing the same job, not to mention that fact that I was still wearing short pants. Was this what quitting to succeed really means, was life just a big game of snakes and ladders, had I landed on that large snake that takes you all the way back to the start?

On the plus side the letters of threat from the taxman had stopped, the money wasn't fantastic, but it was a regular weekly income. As I approached the New Year I realised that I had to simply accept my circumstances and started to focus on the plus side.

I simply swallowed my pride and got on with it. After all I had a job, which still gave me the flexibility to do other things. I enrolled at the local college to finally complete the PTTLS course, something I should have done years ago. This was without doubt the turning point in beating depression.

Chapter 11

Education, Education, Education

Tony Blair quite famously said his three priorities while in office were education, education, education. Although this is not in any way a political rant I personally realised that education was and still is without doubt one of the single most important factors in my life today. Although I am a long way off becoming a true academic, as I am yet to complete a degree let alone a PhD. Perhaps Tony Blair was right to focus his attention on education. I remember while working temporarily at Newcastle University, which was not that long after this infamous speech and not that long before I left the Army. There seemed to be a big push in getting people from deprived backgrounds into university.

As a kid I never really excelled at school, I am sure I could have done much better if I was encouraged. I suppose like most kids growing up in the late sixties to mid-seventies it never seemed to be that important. I don't remember being encouraged to stay on. I couldn't wait to leave. When people ask me what I did at school all I remember from my primary school years where the times we spent running around the playground with our arms round each other's shoulders shouting, *"all join on for Cowboys and Indians"* it started with just two of us until the line gradually grew as other kids joined in with our hypnotic chant. We never actually played cowboys and Indians despite our enthusiasm to get people to join us, by the time we had enough of us to play break time was over. The other major pastime was running up and down the mountain of coke, a lightweight coal like substance which was used as fuel for the school boiler room. I remember once making it to the top, just as the caretaker opened the chute to the boiler room. I was sucked under and slid towards the fiery furnace, to the applause from my fellow pupils. The caretaker got the shock of his life when he saw some crazy kid hurtling towards him. These were certainly not the skills required for the eleven plus. And going to Grammar School was only something the posh kids did, not some scruffy skinny kid from a council estate with a strange coke habit.

My time at secondary school wasn't that much different, the latter years seemed to be spent waiting for the bell to ring, or playing cards in the common room. We just took school for granted in those days; it was just somewhere we went during the day. Nonetheless I did sit all my exams, Maths, English, Geography and Science. One subject I did love at the time was Technical Drawing, as it required a degree of perfection, something I later discovered to be one of my primary characteristics'. I was a bit of a perfectionist, which is believed to be quite commonly associated with anxiety, depression and procrastination.

Psychologists believe that there is a strong connection between these characteristic. I would often put things off if I knew I could not do them perfectly. I am sure we all experience this by simply having to wait for the right moment before we attempt something, or not at all because it won't be right, or possibly result in failure.

I was without doubt a true perfectionist. You just have to ask my wife. Especially when she found me ripping up the laminate flooring I had just spent all weekend laying, following a visit from my brother in law. Who had quietly told her that it should be running down the length of the room and not laid horizontally as I had done. Apparently it was something to do with the light from the windows. I suppose this is similar to the common DIY crime as hanging wallpaper upside-down.

I was not the best at DIY something I will freely admit, but this was a real blow as I had on this occasion purchased all the right tools for the job, cut each piece to perfection, using the old adage/saying, measure twice cut once. I stood there on completion of this task with my arms out wide, like a demented Laurence Luellen Bowan at the end of one of those makeover shows, saying what do you think of that then love? She still wonders why I hate the weekend visits to B&Q and cringe when we walk past the laminate section.

At my lowest point I never thought going back to sit in a classroom would help to cure my feelings of depression, but it did. Enrolling for the PTTLS course gave me a purpose, something to achieve. Once a week for an eleven week period I took off my Royal Mail uniform and sat amongst a class of adult learners, all from different backgrounds, all with a different story to tell. It's funny looking back that I never actually told any of them that I was just a humble postman, it actually didn't matter. What we were all interested to know was what subject we were going to teach at the end of the course. This course also helped me to refocus my attention on what I was really good at. By the end of the course I had written a full course programme, syllabus and produced all the materials needed to teach all aspects of web design. Giving me all the tools needed to take someone from a complete beginner to way beyond intermediate level in web creation, design and marketing.

My recovery from depression was well underway. The time sat back in the van with my fellow posties gave me something else to talk about. Most of the time prior to my new found passion I would simply join in the conversation about mail related topics, which was mainly a moan about how many parcels we had to deliver, and how shit the walk was. Many of my fellow colleagues were old school posties, from the days when finishing times were once mid mornings, rather than late afternoon. I am not saying that it was all moans and groans, but it did seem the favourite pastime for most. Each to their own as the saying goes. I was now happy being a postman, although still not sure for how much longer. I was still on a rolling contract and the hours suited me, as I had time to think.

It was during this time that I first thought about writing this book. I had had similar thoughts before, but this time it was different. I did struggle for a while though, wondering what the book would be about, was it simply an autobiography, or a self-help book, who would I be helping? Writing was not a problem as my previous course work was mainly essay based, so I was now used to sitting back down in front of the keyboard again. My problem like many I am sure, was that feeling of doubt, can I actually do this, what will people say if I tell them I am writing a book?

It's funny how easy self-doubt enters our heads. I am sure I have read or heard somewhere that part of the cure for depression is to stop worrying about what others think. It's a fact that very few people are thinking about you anyway, well certainly those outside your immediate family. So why do we worry what other people think.

Chapter 12

On Reflection

Looking back over that period from when I left the Army to the time of sitting down and starting to write this book, I am so glad that I made the effort. Although this period in my life at times seems like a distant memory, it has flown by, if that makes sense? When I first thought about writing this book my main concern and constant excuse for not writing, was that I was not yet successful. I had not yet reached what I would term any great level of success. Although success is measured differently, as we all have our own views on what success means to us personally.

The real truth of the matter is, I have learned so much about myself, as I am starting to see the person I really am. Most autobiographies are written by successful people, those we know through media or have achieved so called celebrity status for whatever reason. Having read a number of these main stream celebrity autobiographies, their life before they became famous was not that much different than any of us. We all face the same problems and challenges in life.

Although I enjoyed reading some of these books, there were times when I thought that perhaps these books are just a cry for attention, very few books of this nature make any real money. So are they simply a promotional tool. I suppose this is quite evident especially as we approached the Christmas period and every man and his dog has a book to promote.

On every chat show during the run up to festive season someone will be plugging a book. Perhaps the outcome of this book will pose the same question, is this my own personal cry for attention? I can think of lots of reasons for writing this book, but maybe it's just the fact that I want to prove that I can start and finish a project.

Whatever your thoughts maybe, I can fully recommend that time spent on reflection is well worth it, and writing it down and making it tangible is even more so. Understandably we all at one time or another think back to relevant points in our lives, some wait for that moment when it flashes before their eyes, quite often this can be too late. I have found that writing a book encourages you to take stock of who we are, although this is not the end of this particular book I only thought it right to add this chapter, on reflection as I focus my thoughts on its completion.

When I first set out on this journey I simply thought that the period which I needed to reflect on most where those years after leaving the Army. Having now got to this point in the book I now feel I have to revisit much more of my life to fully understand the person I am and to complete my own psychoanalysis of my life so far.

The previous chapters have helped me to understand where I went wrong, in the next section I will explore my memories of childhood, adolescence and more of my time in the Army to help me to find the real me. It's funny that we often hear that phrase, but what do we actually mean when we say, I need to find myself, find the real me?

The Best Loser

I don't know why but I have always thought of myself as a Joe average. I was never really the best at anything; I played quite a lot of sport in the Army but was never the best player. Although I know I wasn't just someone who made up the numbers, I am sure I made a valuable contribution, but I often simply blended into the background. I suppose the best loser accolade sums me up. Perhaps when I reach the end of this book I will have found the real me.

Chapter 13

My Earliest Memories

Some people say they can remember things from way back in their childhood, experts say many of us can only remember snippets from our early childhood especially between the years of 3 to 7. When I started to sit down and write this section of the book I too searched my memory bank and found it quite true, it was hard to remember things during those infant years, and I too was suffering from what is known as infantile amnesia.

My earliest memory as a three year old kid, and I am not quite sure how or why this memory has stayed with me. Because for a long time I actually thought this was a dream, that's until it was confirmed by my mum many years later.

I remember waking up in the early hours of the morning and walking downstairs, it was close to Christmas 1963, just less than a month from my fourth birthday. I remember walking on the cold wooden floor on the stairs, due to the fact that we never actually had a stair carpet, apparently quite common back in the early sixties. I remember seeing rows of big silver galvanised buckets, filled to the brim with fruit, apples, oranges, pears, all standing in rows at the bottom of the stairs. (*I know that rhymes but it's very true*).

This was quite strange as the only bucket we had was normally on the landing, which was used as an indoor loo, and emitted an odour far from that associated with sweet smelling fruit. I know we weren't alone as many people I grew up with often talked about the bucket at the top of the stairs, and quite possibly one of the reasons why very few people had a stair carpet. Due to them constantly being kicked over on the landing by drunken dads returning home from the pub after dark, resulting in the contents cascading down the stairs like something from a scene on the log flume at Alton Towers.

My mum told me that my dad was given the fruit for doing a job, not quite sure what the job was, but I later discovered that my dad was a bit of a lad, as they say, and not long after that spent some time at Her Majesties pleasure at Strangeways in Manchester. Not for nicking fruit, he had his sights set on a slightly higher prize and got pinched for robbing the local rent office.

When I was four years old I remember quite vividly visiting him, when I think back to this period I can picture quite clearly a seesaw which both me and our Mick played on while mum went to talk to dad and show him his new born son. I remember the long bus ride, which seemed to take us all day to get there. This was just a few weeks after my younger brother Paddy was born in April 1964.

Prior to his pending birth along with my elder brother Mick and young sister Sharon we spent a short time in a children's home. I was four, Mick was Six and Sharon was just two years old. This short spell was due to that fact that my dad was serving his time, mum had been rushed into hospital to give birth to our younger brother. We only spent a few days in this home before we were rescued by relatives. Fortunately my dad had a large family who had rallied round to get us out of the home. I went to stay with my auntie Annie and Uncle Jack who had a large pub in Chadderton, Mick stayed with auntie Norah and Sharon with auntie Kath. I remember that at the time my right arm was in a sling and in a plaster cast.

This is quite possibly why I remember this time in my life, again so vividly. It was my mum who actually broke my arm, she didn't do it deliberately, apparently we had to go somewhere and I was sitting in a chair refusing to get up and put my coat on, like any typical stubborn four year old I had my own agenda. My mum was no doubt heavily pregnant at the time, my dad was in prison, and this little sod is refusing to co-operate. She yanked my arm to get me out of the chair to get me dressed, which resulted in a broken arm, ouch! (*I forgive you mum*).

One other memory that remains vivid was also from this period, when we lived in the old two up two down on the end of a cobbled street in Oldham. Leech Street, it's gone now, but back then it was a typical Northern narrow street, with back to back houses. The opposite side of the house was flanked by a high stone wall, which made the street dark. I also remember the old gas lamp lighting that ran down the length of this dark street. It was very cold in that house during the winter months. I can actually remember that ice formed on the inside of the windows in winter. An incident I remember very well was in the summer of 1964, I was jumping off a small wall which was just opposite the house and ran parallel at an angle to the large wall. It was a warm whit Sunday and we had just finished having our photos taken. I was dressed in my Whit Sunday best and we were waiting to take the long two and half mile walk to Lees to see our aunties and uncles. For those who remember these times it meant that we would get a Threepenny Bit or a shiny Sixpence for looking smart in our new clothes and shoes, which always rubbed on the back of your heels all the way there and back again. But we never complained it was worth the Sixpence.

Visiting our aunties in Lees was something we did for years after; at least until the age of ten. We would meet up with all our cousins, at Aunty Maggie's and Uncle Fred's house, my dad's eldest sister. I remember the house being immaculate inside and the garden at the back with roses. Aunty Maggie was the typical matriarch figure, most definitely a Mrs Bucket (bouquet) type of character. One of his other sisters, Aunty Kath was the landlady of the Devonshire pub across the road on Johns Street in Lees. We never went in the pub, as it wasn't something kids did back then, unlike today you can't move for screaming kids and pushchairs in pubs on Sunday afternoon these days, well at least the ones that haven't been turned into a convenient store or one of those anything for a pound shops. Although the Devonshire pub survived and still exists today, albeit under different name, as its now a trendy wine bar called, the Milan.

So back to this particular whit Sunday... One of the games me and Mick would play was to walk along the smaller wall that got higher as you walked down the hill and jump off on to the cobbles below. I would regularly jump off this small wall without hesitation, I would always go that little bit further than him, I was fearless. Unfortunately on this occasion, on landing feet first I fell forward face first and smashed my top lip on a broken piece of glass. I remember the blood that seemed to fill the washing bowl as I lay on my mums lap while she held a cold wet flannel to my face. I don't remember going to hospital or having any stitches, just the cold wet flannel, which quite possibly had the healing powers of the magic sponge. The same healing powers of the cold key on a piece of string placed on your back during a nose bleed, or the butter that she would apply to a lump on your forehead or was it margarine, as we could never afford butter.

One thing I do know is that this episode left me without the sixpence as we never made that trip to Lees, not forgetting a permanent scar on my top lip which was often mistaken for two ink marks and is visible on all my childhood pictures. It's funny that most of my early childhood memories involve some kind of accident or injury; blood and broken bones.

Chapter 14

Fearless

We moved from the cold dark house on Leech Street to a house slightly bigger on the main Huddersfield Road in Waterhead. It wasn't that far from the old house as it was literally on the other side of the large wall that ran down the length of Leech Street.

Huddersfield Road was a busy main road, although there weren't as many cars on the road back in 1965, it was on a major bus route and the windows would vibrate every time one went past the house. We spent five years in this house. My mum worked as a cleaner at the Sheppard's Boy pub just down the road, opposite what once was the main bus terminus for the 82 and 98 buses that ran from Waterhead to Manchester. My dad was a Turner by trade and worked on a lathe at various local engineering firms. Unfortunately he seemed to have difficulty staying at a firm for long and was often in and out of work, although we didn't notice, as we didn't see much of him during the day, he was always out seeing a man about a dog.

I started school at the age of five and went to the same school as our Mick, St Anne's Roman Catholic Primary School, which was on Cow Lane in Oldham before it was knocked down and re-built on Greenacers Road in the late 80's. It was also the same school my dad went to in the 30's with Bernard Cribbins, the actor.

I remember it was a long walk to school especially during bad weather, which was most of the time, for us Northern folk. I am sure I wore wellies (Wellington Boots) all year round. Like most kids I had chapped legs, two distinctive red rings just below the knee. Rain or shine we would all wear our welly bobs. I remember I would hang on to my mum's coat tails as she pushed the big pram along the busy main road with baby Paddy and three year old Sharon snuggled inside. I remember that first day at school; I can still feel the tightness of the itchy round neck striped jumper that made me feel hot and sticky, it was one of our Mick's hand me downs that shrunk in the wash. Not forgetting the short pants, these were compulsory until you reached big school, hence the chapped legs due to the constant rubbing of rubber wellies against the bare flesh on your legs. I think I started school a few weeks after the other kids in my class, because I remember having to sit in the middle of the room while I was introduced to all the other kids. I had been off at the start of term with asthma. A condition I eventually grew out of, but it was quite bad at times especially during the earlier years before my mid-teens. I remember that simply walking upstairs to bed was difficult at times and left me wheezing like an eighty year old sucking on a Capstan full strength.

It wasn't long before it was big brother Mick's duty to ensure I got to school and home again, although there was only two years between us that age gap seemed much bigger when you are a young kid. We never actually played together much, but because he was older I was allowed to venture further from the house as long as I was with him, and within shouting distance. For those not familiar with this natural unit of measurement, it's the distance you can hear your mum shout from the front step. Like sheep calling to their new born lambs, there is no mistaking your own mothers call. "**Michael! Mark! Your Tea's Ready!**" We could be miles away on a hillside and still hear these cries, like two Meerkats we would immediately stop whatever it was we were doing, even our friends would stand in silence ... was that your mum?

As a kid I was at times a bit of a loner, despite having three other siblings in the family I would often prefer my own company. My other childhood companion was a dog called Ginty, I suppose that man my dad went to see eventually came up with the goods. Ginty was named after a Val Doonican song my dad used to sing titled "Paddy McGinty's Goat". I remember the day we collected him from the RSPCA dog's home on Rochdale Road. I carried him all the way home under my coat. He followed me everywhere after that. Until the day he was hit by a bus on Huddersfield road, he survived the impact but was badly injured and had to be put down. So in less than two years and we were heading back to the RSPCA to have him destroyed. I never wanted another dog after that experience, you get to know them, love then and then they go and die on you. So at the age of seven I had decided I would rather be on my own.

Like most young kids growing up in the mid-sixties and seventies we always seemed to find places to explore. At the age of seven I decided to venture out on my own and walked to the quarry to find the giants' foot print, my other friends had gone home and I was left to find it on my own. Prior to my lone adventure we had been there a few days earlier but never found it. The quarry was part of an old disused rifle range used by the Territorial Army. The so called giant's foot print the object of myth and legend, was nothing more than a large shoe shaped indent that someone had carved into the face of the rocks. My solo journey meant I was way beyond the shouting distance and well and truly in trouble. This was during the long six week summer holidays so it was still light and I had no sense of what time it was. Then I saw a head scarfed figure coming towards, fortunately one of my friends had told my mum where I had gone. She was going ballistic, then came the phrase when you know that pain is about to vibrate through your body, "**come here you little SOD!**" I think the hand prints where still visible on my arse weeks later. My sister still has memories of this incident although she was only five or six at the time and accompanied my mum while she left our Mick to keep an eye on Paddy, not sure where my dad was perhaps seeing another man about a dog. So I was glad it was only my mum I had to confront on that day.

Little did I know at the time that just a few months earlier notorious Moors Murderers Moira Hindley and Ian Brady were active close to where we lived, so at the time I didn't truly understand why my crime was so serious? As a parent and now a grandfather I can fully understand what I must have put her through, and the smacks on my arse where well justified, but kids never see the danger do they.

This was not the first time I tested my mums resolve, a few weeks later I was with my friend throwing stones into the stream close to the waterworks behind the bus terminus, about a mile from the house. I walked down the steep bank to get a larger rock, and as I stood up to walk back up the bank just as he threw his stone, it hit me in the centre of my forehead and like a scene from David and Goliath I went down like a sack of....

I immediately felt the blood running down my face, my friend instinctively ran off in fear, leaving me to walk home covered in blood. As I walked up Huddersfield Road I remember passing people, but no one stopped, fortunately I met our Mick who had been sent to find me, when he saw me he ran back to the house screaming Mum! Marks covered in blood, without hesitation out came the magic flannel once again to mop up the blood. It wasn't as bad as it first seemed and no stitches or infirmary visit was needed. She simply applied margarine to the large bump that had now formed in the centre of my forehead, like something from a Tom & Jerry cartoon. I am not sure why margarine or butter on a bump or as I said earlier a cold key on the back of your neck when suffering from a nose bleed became remedies for these ailments, strange as it may sound they seemed to work, perhaps it is similar to the placebo effect, in that doing something is better than nothing.

Although I never had any major accidents as a kid I did came pretty close. We played in some dangerous places. One of our other areas of play was the derelict houses behind our house. There was lots of renovation going on during the late sixties and early seventies and playing in and around old houses, disused mills, building sites, offered kids like us an exciting place to play, better than any theme park or adventure playground could offer.

I loved climbing when I was a kid and would run along the top of the roofs accessed by the old skylights. While I was up there my dad used to shout, "hey Mark while you are up there lad get the lead". (*Sorry just made that bit up*). There never seemed to be any fear I just remember that I enjoyed looking down on things. Being high had a completely different meaning back then.

One day we discovered the tunnel that went under the two large mills at the bottom of Greenacres Road which are still standing today, the Majestic and Cairo mill, home of the industrial giant Ferranti. The tunnel was dark wet and dangerous and full of killer rats, perfect for young explorers. Let's see where it goes? Was one of the suggestions from someone with a big gob. Before we knew it we were knee deep in water, wading through the dark tunnel, the walls were slimy and cold, we seemed to be down there for hours before we could see a pinpoint of daylight at the other end.

The tunnel was about 400 or 500 metres long, which is a long way when you are a kid crawling around in the dark. At the end of which was a whole new playground know as Manor Flats, this was our very own Narnia. The place we spent most of the summer months jumping the stream building dams lighting grass fires, catching frogs, stickleback fish and red bellied newts, no doubt we were partly responsible for their decline.

There was also a landfill site basically a large tip, where we would find some great stuff especially old pram wheels and bits of bikes, it was a great place for supplies. One day we found an old tractor tyre and rolled it to the top of the steepest hill we could find. We spent hours pushing it to the top, then someone suggested that it would be a great idea if one of us got inside the tyre while we watched it roll back down the hill. Guess who was the smallest, and fitted nicely inside it? Fuck off! I'm not doing it, I know I'm fearless but I'm not fucking crazy, go on think about the £250.00 quid, **WHAT?**

I often think that if we lived in the era of the viral video culture of today we would have made loads of money capturing on film all the crazy things we did back then.

Mum and Dad on their wedding day.

Mum and Dad, me on mums knee just a few weeks old, with big brother Mick, somewhere in Glasgow, on the Clyde 1960.

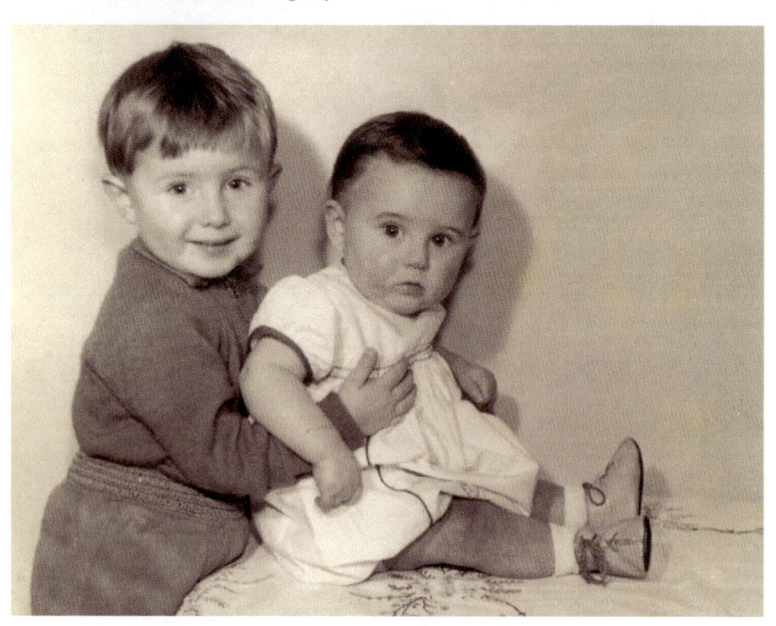

My Big brother Mick looking after me. 1960

Me and Mick outside our house on **Whit Sunday 1964**, *"Mick are you wearing my jacket"*? Just after this photo I jumped off the wall and smashed my face in. See Page 103.

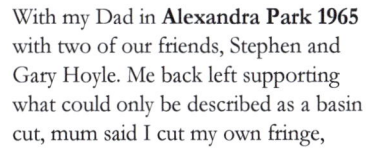

With my Dad in **Alexandra Park 1965** with two of our friends, Stephen and Gary Hoyle. Me back left supporting what could only be described as a basin cut, mum said I cut my own fringe,

Whit Sunday 1966, with some of our cousins at the back of aunty Maggie's house on St Johns Street in Lees, Oldham.

Our Micks at the back laughing in-between two girls, Sharon is the cute one with the basket, baby brother Paddy front left, ready to do a runner. I'm the smart one front right, thinking "we are only doing this photo for the money aren't we?".

113

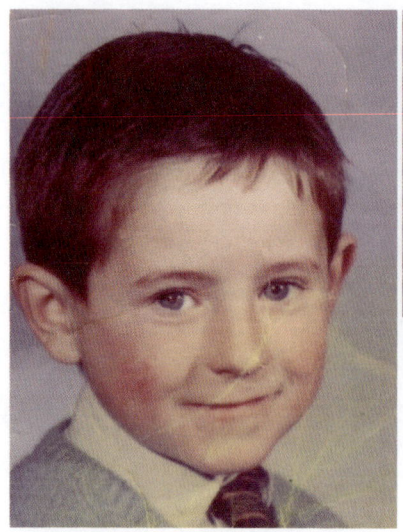

Me and Sharon St Anne's School photo 1968 I think, looks like I cut my own hair again.

Me aged 6 or 7, with my butter wouldn't melt look.

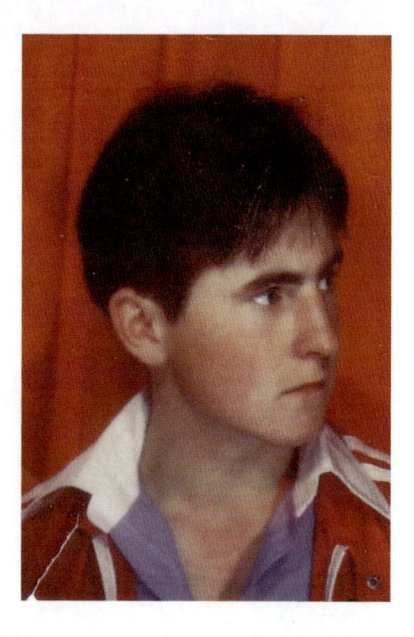

This was me at the age of 16 and the day I joined the Army 14th Sep 1976.

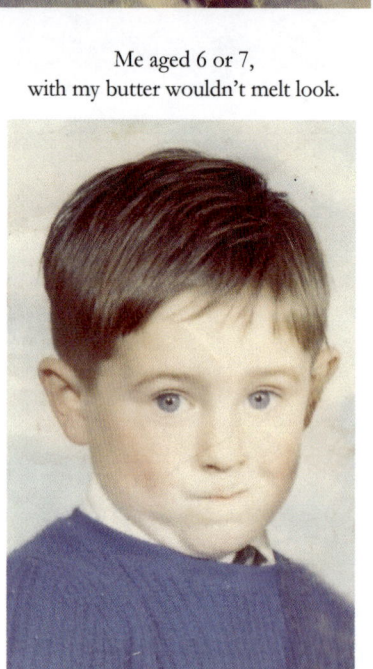

No I'm not smiling, not until I've finished this toffee I'm sucking.

IJLB 1976-77

Yes that's me front centre with Mick Reed to my right, as you look at the picture, picture courtesy of Mick Reed.

Albuhera Company 1976-77
Infantry Junior Leaders Battalion (IJLB)
Not quite sure what we were doing, but I'm
on the floor with my eyes closed?

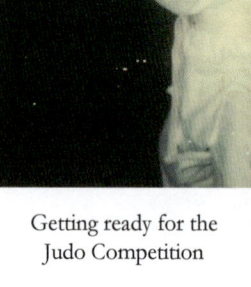

Getting ready for the
Judo Competition

Com on then lets have you!
A few hours later I broke my
collar bone.

L/R Tony Bibby (from Bolton), Scouse Rimmer, Me in the centre and Geordie White on the right. Good memories. Picture courtesy of Mick Reed.

116

UN Tour Cyprus 1978: L/R Jaws, Gaz Walker, Keith Hoo, John Dean (Cess), Me, Geoff Lewins, and there is always one you cant remember, sorry mate..

Standing outside Bravo 25, Me, Cess and the best man at my wedding Griff

117

At just 19 years old we decided to get married

on the 7th July 1979

Linda has still got that decoration from the top of the cake,
and the knife just in case.

JNCOS CADRE MINDEN GERMANY 1979
Top: Me front row centre looking cool with my hand on my chin.
Bottom: The first rung of the promotion ladder begins,
as I am promoted to Lance Corporal.

Authors Note: Sadly many of the photos taken of me during my career have been lost in transit, some of those that survived are published in this book.

BAOR
BATTLE FIELD SURVIVAL

This is to certify that

24433098 CPL M T MOONEY

has successfully completed the

BAOR BATTLE FIELD SURVIVAL

At the

INTERNATIONAL LRRP SCHOOL
UK NATIONAL ELEMENT

from 12 - 23 July 1982

Chief Instructor

I had a great experience with some SAS heroes, at the Long Range Reconnaissance Patrol School Germany in the summer of 1982.

Chapter 15

Moving House

We remained in the house on Huddersfield Road until I was nine years old before we moved to number 30 Redgrave Street a bigger three bed roomed terraced house with a large attic which I shared with big brother Mick. This was much better than living on the main road in Waterhead, although we still had no inside toilet or bathroom. The bath was still the old tin bath type; the toilet was outside in our own backyard. It was the old tippler toilet, a museum piece in its own right. A dark brown ceramic cylinder shape toilet with an old heavy wooden seat.

Apparently researchers say that on average we spend at least 20 minutes a day going to the toilet, so it's no wonder why my memory of this particular one has stayed with me so vividly. For the first few months of using it I would hang on to the sides of the seat in fear of falling through the large hole into the sewer some feet below. When you did a poo there would be a long pause before you heard it hit the water below, there was never any fear of splash back in those days. Going there at night or during the winter months was a real test of courage. Not only was it dark and cold, we were told that rats would climb up and bite you on the arse.

The other main features of the backyard were the coal bunker and the outhouse, where my dad kept all his tools. This later became my very own bike workshop. One of the reasons I remember the coal bunker was due to the fact that

I loved the open coal fire we had in the kitchen/come backroom. Sometimes we would have coal delivered by the coalman but more often than not me and our Mick would have to go to the local shop to buy a bag of coal and carry it all the way back to the house.

Just outside the back gate of the house was a large piece of waste ground, an open space we all called the Croft. This was our football pitch, cycle track, meeting place, the place where we would build large bonfires in November. Collecting the wood for bonfire (*bonny*), started weeks before, as the wood was in endless supply from the derelict houses close by, we had great fun as ripped up floorboards and removed all the internal doors from every house we gained access to. We would carry the doors on our backs, it was like seeing a line of ants carrying leaves back to the nest. As the 5th of November approached collecting wood for the bonny became very competitive, and we would go out on raids to steal wood from other bonfires, or spend the night guarding ours from the dawn raids from other gangs, I say gangs but we were just groups of kids.

One summer the council dumped a large pile of fine gravel which was going to be used to cover the croft to even it out before adding a new play area swings and stuff at the far end. We had better ideas for this mountain of gravel. We dug a huge hole in it, lined it with polythene sheets and built a swimming pool, well that was the intention. We filled it by running a huge length of industrial hose pipe from Peter Garlick's kitchen, as his house was the closest. It went through the house and across Beresford Street to the large hole, fortunately his mum and dad were out at the time. We borrowed the hose pipe, large polythene sheets and the sand from the building site, well that's what we told the police/local bobby when all the residents came out on Beresford Street due to that fact that they now had no water because we had it running all day and had apparently effected the water pressure or something.

The large building site just beyond the Croft was another area of 1970's redevelopment. I am sure we delayed this project for a few years as we seemed to borrow lots of stuff from the site, everything from tubs of putty to copper wiring, which we cut up and used as ammunition for our elastic catapults'. We would bend the wire into a U shape and fire them at milk bottles or each other. Elastic was never in short supply as just across the street from where we lived on Redgrave Street was Oldham Elastic Works, this is where my mum worked for a while before it closed down in the mid Seventies.

From the age of nine to eleven playing in derelict houses seemed to be where I spent most of my time. I remember one particular day we found an electric meter, in those days almost everyone paid for their gas and electricity on the Shilling meter, 5p in today's money. My dad made a key for ours and one for the black and white telly which also had its own money box. And people today think pay for view is a new concept. My dad's key cutting skills were no doubt acquired as a Turner and lathe operator or perhaps something he picked up during his brief visit at Her Majesties Pleasure. I'm not quite sure how long he got away with it, but when the telly man came to collect his money and found just four tanners (Sixpences) in the box, my dad told him that there was never anything on so we didn't watch it that often.

So this particular meter box we had found was a potential money maker if we could smash it open and get the money out. What we didn't know was that the mains were still connected and this sucker was still live! To this day I don't know why none of us weren't killed at the time. We would take turns in picking it up and receiving a shock. It was like one of those crazy Japanese TV Kamikaze shows, as we challenged each other to see who could hold on to it for the longest. At one point we all held hands while the person on the end held on to the meter and the electricity passed through all of us. Its funny when I see people on Blackpool prom paying to sit in that chair that gives you a shock when you hold on to those metal rods on the arms of the chair. We did that for free back in 1970.

The other crazy things we did included building a den from the doors we collected from the derelict houses. We would nail them together to create a large box shaped structure, basically a tree house without the tree. That's not crazy thing, but sitting inside it while we lit fireworks was lunacy, we would sit in circle with a Volcano firework erupting just a few feet away, not the best environment for an asthma sufferer. It's amazing that no one was seriously injured.

The most dangerous stunt was when we would build a large fire on the croft and find empty five gallon containers, or old paint tins from the building site, in which we would add a small amount of diesel as this was never in short supply, it was fuel for the dumper trucks left on the building site over the weekend. We would throw the container on the fire and stand around waiting for it to explode. Little did I know that less than ten years later I would be facing a much more lethal form of blast incendiary? Perhaps this was great conditioning for things to come.

Living on Redgrave Street also meant that we were now closer to school which was now only a short five or ten minute walk away. Going to a Catholic School also meant that going to church on Sunday was compulsory. This was back in the day when there was a Mass 3 or 4 times on Sunday's. On occasion we would go as a family especially during the big events on the Catholic calendar, Ash Wednesday, Palm Sunday, First communion, Confirmation, but more often than not I would go with our Mick. We would be given a couple of pennies or a sixpence for the collection, which quite often never made it to the collection plate. We would set off for church at 10 30am dressed in our Sunday best to make it in time for the 11 O'clock Mass. More often than not we would walk the extra mile down Balfour Street, along Lees Road to Aunty Norah's and Uncle Albert's house at No 5 Brewerton Road.

We had no intention of going to church we could double our money by paying a visit to our Aunty, who would always ask if we had been to church? "Yes of course we have, we went to ten O'clock mass", there was always another sixpence to be gained or a piece of cake, and sweets

The Best Loser

when visiting my dad's older sister. One of the other reasons for going was that we got to play with the toys uncle Albert had bought for my cousin Christine, apparently he always wanted a boy and bought the toys before she was born.

One of my favourite toys was a large green Army Tank that fired rockets. We never had anything like this at our house. At Christmas we always got the same thing, although as I recall it did come in a large box, and I am sure most people my age can remember the excitement of opening a COMPENDIUM OF GAMES. From the age of seven to the age of ten it was always the same, understandably the excitement wore off after a while.

The large box contained the popular board games, Snakes and Ladders, Ludo, Draughts, and Tiddlywinks. So getting the chance to play with actual toys was a real joy. I'm not saying that we weren't grateful for what we had we actually didn't know any different during those earlier years.

Although we had lots of Aunties and Uncles on my dad's side of the family, Uncle Albert was my favourite uncle and later became one of my mentors, I also worked with him for a while before I joined the army. He ran his own plumbing and building business, he also worked for Ferranti, and I later discovered that he was also a former Worshipful Master of the Hyde Freemason Lodge. The best way to describe him would be to compare him to the Doc Brown character from Back to the Future played by Christopher Lloyd. He was always making something in his workshop, later in life he actually became more like the Uncle Albert character in Only Fools and Horses, due to the stories he would tell about his days in the Army... *"During the war..."* Although I had heard the stories many times before, I found him to be a real character, he achieved so much in his life. I suppose deep down I wished that I could have had similar conversation with my dad.

30 Redgrave Street was our final family home where we were all together before tragedy stuck. I have lots of fond memories from this period in my life, and until I sat down to write this particular section of the book I never actually knew how lucky I was back then. Although it was at this house where my life changed forever, especially on that Saturday morning in October 1974, understandably it was the place that shaped my future.

Chapter 16

Big School, New Friends

&

Free Dinners

In September 1971 I started my secondary school education and going to school was once again a daily trek. Although there were buses to school we found it quicker to walk over Glodwick Lows to Abbey Hills, rather than catch two buses. To be honest the real truth is that we very rarely had money for the bus anyway, especially during the first two years, so walking was the only option we had. St Albans school was on Warren Lane, sadly it's long gone, as it would be nice to be able to pay a visit and walk the corridors that joined the two main sections of the school. I'm slightly envious when I see celebrities revisiting their old schools, meeting teachers, getting a chance to sit at the old desk. It's funny that when we were there we couldn't wait to reach sixth form and leave. If only we knew then what we know now?

I remember that first day; long trousers school blazer, white shirt, tie, green jumper, new shoes. All our Mick's hand me downs apart from the shoes, they were new and hurt like hell for a few weeks. Uniform wasn't compulsory as far as I can remember as we only seemed to wear it during that first year. I suppose the thing most of us remember from this time in our lives is how big the schools seemed to be, not to mention the number of kids, there seemed to hundreds of us. Although there were some familiar faces from primary school I seemed to be in class of total strangers.

I was actually a quiet kid, to say I was a bit shy was probably an understatement. I don't think I spoke to anyone on that first day. I actually don't remember much from that first year, but by the end of the second year I had quite a large circle of friends, well I say friends, kids I hung around with at break times and lunchtime. The kids I later played truant with when we couldn't be bothered to go back after the lunchtime break. I suppose like most of us we had two main groups of friends, those we shared the same classroom with, and those that lived within a small radius of our homes.

It was also at this time when I discovered that we were poorer than some of the other kids in my class, not because of the clothes they wore. This was something that was evident when it came to meal times. For the first few years at school like most kids I attended school dinners, and with my blue dinner ticket in my hand clearly marked with the word FREE, I joined the dinner queue with all the other scruffs and the paupers. I wasn't the only one in my class; there were a number of us in the free school dinner gang. We were the Oliver's, *"please miss can I have some more?"*. We were the ones that the dinner ladies took pity on, who would ask, how many potato scoops do you want luv? Or who wants the skin off the custard? The other kids would push in front of you in fear that there would be nothing left when

129

they reached the hot plate. It wasn't until the third year when we ventured out to buy our own school dinner from the Jolly Fryer on Abbey Hills Road, a meat pie or a chip muffin was the staple diet of a thirteen year old. I think my dad was back in work during this time as we no longer qualified for free school dinners.

By this time I had also started smoking, not the best addiction for a kid with a history of asthma. I would tell my mum that I was now catching the bus to school, as this would give me just enough money with what she also gave us for our dinner, to have enough to buy Five Park Drive Tipped and a Penny Book of Matches, and still have enough for a chip muffin. It's funny that we were never questioned or challenged about who the fags were for in those days. Today kids under the age of 18 need to be master forgers to obtain cigarettes over the counter, requiring false passports, and photo ID.

We could buy anything without question from the local shop when we were growing up, more often than not on tick, the slate; all we needed was a note from your mum or dad. If we were lucky we would also be given oddy (pocket money). I suppose this was a word relating to the odd coppers dads would have in their pockets when they came home from work on Friday.

This oddy helped to support our new smoking habit, however more often than not my dad would arrive home late on Friday night worse for wear, which was no doubt drink related, and would fall asleep in the chair, so no oddy was given out on those occasions.

There was one particular occasion when me and our Mick decided to take matters into our own hands. After returning home drunk my dad would leave his work trousers on the end of his bed. So one night Mick decided we should take matters into our own hands. I was the younger kid so I was the one who had to sneak in and take some change out of his pockets, while Mick stood on the landing keeping look out just in case mum came up. I crawled along the floor like a ninja avoiding the motion sensors, these were in fact the squeaky floor boards, and the sideboard that had big metal draw handles on it that rattled when you walked past it. The bed was one of those big old double beds with a large solid wooden headboard, and the end of the bed was a heavy solid wooden bed end, which helped to conceal my sneaky approach. When I reached the bed I had to kneel up to reach into his trouser pockets.

The first pocket I tried was empty, the other one was heavy and bulging with change I could also feel paper. The intention was to just grab a few coppers but this was too noisy so I slowly pulled on a piece of paper scrunching it in my hand before withdrawing it and scuttling back across the floor to the landing and then up the next flight of stairs to our attic bedroom. How much did you get? I don't know, I think I got a ten bob note? I opened my hand the crumpled piece of paper slowly unfolded like a flower in the morning sun, only to reveal a crisp new five pound note. Shit what are we going to do with that? There was no way we could put this back.

I felt bad at first, this was stealing, a mortal sin, at least ten Hail Marys at the next confessional. Then this feeling of guilt started to subside as my memory of that seventh birthday came flooding back, I was only taking what was rightfully mine after that potato stunt he pulled, when I was seven. So I didn't feel as bad anymore.

The next day we went to the shop to spend our crisp five pound note. We both bought 20 Number Six, this was my first ever packet of 20 cigarettes, plus an endless supply of sweets and for some strange reason we bought a rugby ball.

We hid the fags above the top of the door in the outside toilet in the backyard. They lasted for weeks; until that day when my dad just happened to look up above the door when he sat down to do his business. He was slightly taller than us so the cigarettes we thought were out of view were in fact quite clearly on display. It's fair to say that he went mental not because he had finally discovered that we were smoking, he was more angry that he didn't have any cigarettes at the time and we had a stash of snout in the outside toilet. I don't think he ever found out about the fiver, but my mum once told us that no matter how drunk he was he always knew how much he had in his pockets. I think most of us have this skill, we can sometimes forget what we did the night before but ask us what we have in our pockets and we can tell to the last penny.

Although time moves pretty quickly nowadays, when I was at school time seemed to move much slower. The six week summer holidays where long, we seemed to do so much during that period. Although we very rarely went on holiday, in fact we only ever had one family holiday with my mum and dad. This was a week in a caravan at Winkcups Holiday Camp in Colwyn Bay North Wales. I was also allowed to invite my friend Simon Lord (Sash) who lived just up the street. Sash and his older brother Tim were also my cycling buddies. Tim was a year older than us and introduced me to the sport of cycle speedway. Their dad was also mad keen on Speedway and one weekend I went with them to Bell Vue in Manchester to my first ever Speedway meeting. It's fair to say that I was hooked and for the next three years I was a keen supporter of Bell Vue Aces, this was in the days of the famous Ivan Mauger, Peter Collins and Ole Olson, all of which were the riding superstars of the early seventies.

I loved the attraction of speedway, the noise of the engines the smell of the Nitro fumes, the speed the danger. We would position ourselves close to the corners as the bikes skidded out of the bend, at times it felt like we were almost in touching distance as the grit from the track would rain down on us. At the end of the heats we would run on to the track to collect the pieces of Perspex the riders would flick off from their visors. These were a temporary thin visor covers that they attached to the helmet to give them additional visual protection. As you can imagine without this disposable shield in front of the main visor after four laps of the track they would not see anything, especially when it was wet.

After the Speedway meeting we would all get free access to the Amusement Park at Bell Vue where I experienced my first rollercoaster ride. Before long we were all going on our own, we would catch the train from Oldham Mumps train station to Miles Platting and then take a short bus ride to Bell Vue to see our heroes in action. There was one particular weekend when we came very close to serious injury, like many motor sports the crowd also put themselves in danger, and crashes are quite common. The barrier was only about four foot high between spectator and the track. When there was a collision both the bike and the rider would often be catapulted into the crowd. A bike coming off the track at speeds of up to 70mph can do some serious damage, riders have also died as a result. We were just a few feet away from a serious incident once, when the rider hit the barrier and the bike landed in the crowd. I'm not sure how serious the three spectators were injured by the flying bike but the ambulance took them away. We heard later that the rider lost a couple of fingers, however the meeting restarted about 30mins later and we all rushed back to the bend to resume our positions, lightning never strikes twice …eh.

Chapter 17

Bikes and Bogies (Bogey's)

From the age of thirteen there was only one thing I was interested in and that was my bike. The one I saved up for from the money I got paid as a paperboy. By this time the council had now levelled part of the Croft after reclaiming the gravel we had used temporally for our swimming pool. So we now had the perfect surface for our very own cycle Speedway track.

If we weren't on our bikes we were making and riding bogies (*American equivalent, box cart*), down the steepest hill we could find. If we didn't have the wood to build the cart we would use the bottom frame and wheels from an old pram, there were plenty of these on the local tip or just dumped and discarded in the back alleys, due to the introduction of the now popular Maclaren Buggy, as this was now the popular choice of new young mothers in the early 70's.

The heavy old prams with their spring suspension made the perfect downhill death trap. To steer we would simply drag our right or left leg on the ground, undoubtedly this meant that your shoes took a hammering. My mum would often threaten us and say if you wear-out another pair of shoes you'll go to school in a pair of bloody clogs lad. These are not to be confused with the now popular brand name of Clogs® worn by nurses and surgeons, the ones she was threatening us with were the ones worn by mill workers, dinner ladies and Morris Dancers.

Building a proper bogie *(bogey not quite sure of the proper spelling)*, was a skill in itself, although I am not the best at DIY by today's standards. I could build a cracking bogie when I was a kid. Although we never had all the tools for the job as very few people had access to drills and jig saws like they do today. Who needs a drill anyway when there is a much more exciting way to create a hole in a piece of wood? A red hot poker from a roaring coal fire was perfect for creating the holes for the large bolt that joined the body of the bogie to the steering section.

The heavy poker my dad had made at work which had a large heavy knurled brass handle was perfect in every way, the right diameter and the weight of it helped create the perfect hole. When it was almost white hot it would burn through wood like pushing a hot knife through butter. When it snowed we turned our attention to making a sledge, there were lots of places to throw yourself head first down a hill. The place we found most exciting and particularly dangerous was Redgrave Passage. This was a steep cobbled stone hill that ran from the top of Redgrave Street to the busy Huddersfield Road at the bottom. Just a few feet from the bottom was a small narrow ally on the right that ran behind the houses on the main road. The skill was to execute a sharp right turn at the bottom of the hill, otherwise you would miss the entrance and crash into the wall at top speed. Failing that you would continue down the hill and end up in the main road with traffic coming at you from either direction.

Why was it that everything we did back then involved an element of danger, or is that I just remember the crazy stuff we did and not any of the other less adventurous aspects of my childhood. The truth is I was never in the house; we had no need to be, apart from meal times, or when watching the odd Tom & Jerry cartoon on TV. Sitting in the house was something very few of us ever did. If you weren't knocking on someone's door you can guarantee that someone would be knocking on yours asking the immortal question "are you playing out"?

Even when I had bouts of asthma I still wanted to be out of the house, I hated being cooped up. Understandably when it was really bad my mum would keep me confined to the house. During these times of confinement I would help her in the kitchen, most of the time I just watched over her shoulder at first, but it wasn't long before I became a sous chef in my own right, I was definitely second in command in our kitchen.

I suppose it was during these times that I picked up many culinary skills, although we didn't have much money for fancy ingredients' you see on most supermarket shelves, like most mums of the post war era they could make a meal out of almost nothing. I also learned how to make biscuits', shortbread, and flapjacks. Although I didn't know it at the time I learned many domestic science skills from my mum. I helped with the ironing, washing, although I would stay clear of the cleaning if it involved dust as this would only aggravate the asthma. I remember going to the doctors once and my mum was asked if I went swimming, SWIMMING!

The Best Loser

I didn't even have a pair of trunks. But this was soon fixed by my mum… that weekend she went to a jumble sale, she didn't find any trunks but she did find a girls swimming costume, and being a domesticated goddess she cut off the knickers section of the costume to make me my first pair of navy blue swimming trunks. I actually learned to swim quite quickly, I think the philosophy in schools at the time was more like a swim or die technique, before we knew it we were diving to the bottom of the deep end dressed in our pyjamas to rescue a black brick. The only thing I hated about going to the swimming lessons at schools was having to rush to get dresses at the end. When I think about it now I can still smell the chlorine, and can still feel the that sensation of putting socks on wet feet and your shirt sticking to your back because you never had time to dry yourself properly. No wonder so many kids back then got a verruca.

The swimming no doubt helped to strengthen my lungs, the bike riding and paper round I did also helped to keep me fit and active, not that I was aware of it at the time. Nevertheless I was always the one in front when we had to run away for whatever reason especially short distances. During the school sports days I was always in the 100 metres and the relay, but was never the fastest kid, always coming a good second or third. Although I remember I hated cross country, I think most kids did, I don't think we ever completed the course, we would always find a place to hide half way round, wait for them to come round again and then just tag on at the back. It's funny how something you hated as a kid becomes your favourite pastime when you get much older.

Chapter 18

How Things Can Quickly Change

By the age of fourteen I was almost free from my incapacitating bouts of asthma. The bike I built was still my fulltime friend. However I was becoming more aware of music and the biggest influences at the time were David Bowie and Marc Bolan, as people my age witnessed the birth of Glam Rock. Fashion was changing and I like most teenage boys my age we took a little more interest in what we were wearing. The pictures of my speedway idols now shared wall space in my bedroom with Ziggy Stardust and the Spiders from Mars, and staying in on Sunday to listen to the top 40 charts started to become a more regular occurrence.

October 1974 was without doubt the worst time of my adolescent years. Two dates in particular come to mind, Saturday 5th of October was when Oldham's famous Market Hall was burnt to the ground, and the day I was going into town to buy a green star jumper with the money I earned from my paper round. It was devastating to see this iconic building totally gutted. I actually had no idea that it had burnt to the ground during the early hours of that Saturday morning. Although there was a distinctive smell of fire and smoke in the air the type you get on the morning after bonfire night. On that morning, I simply finished my paper round collected my money at 9.30 jumped on a 98 bus, arrived in the town centre to see people just standing around what was once the heart of Oldham's town centre, some were crying. The fire engines were still there it was completely flattened, gone forever. Who would have thought that just three weeks later my own world would be turned upside down?

On Friday 25th of October my dad got ready to go out, this was nothing new, something he did most weekends. As usual he wore a suit and tie, he was a smart looking man, always taking pride in his appearance, with his slicked back Brylcreemed hair, he looked like a young Frank Sinatra. When money was tight he would use liquid paraffin to create that slicked back style and sheen on his thick black hair, (*something I inherited as a teenager but lost in my early twenties*).

On this occasion he was joining his friends on a Stag Night, on their usual local pub crawl, visiting the pubs in Oldham, making their way to the infamous Candlelight Club at the top of the town. I never actually saw him leave that night, it was just another ordinary Friday occurrence. Little did I know that this would be the last time he would leave the house. And little did I know that when I left the house at 6.30am on the following Saturday morning to do my paper round that my dad was already dead. How does a fourteen year old kid deal with something like this? To this day we still don't know the real truth of what happened in the club in the early hours of that Saturday morning, there was an inquest into his death which concluded with a verdict of accidental death as a result of a fall. My mum would often say that we would one day find out what really happened. She was adamant that he was involved in a fight and was thrown down the stairs and smashed his head on a radiator which caused a massive brain haemorrhage, he was just 46 years old. I would have liked to have known more about him, we never had any long chats, there was never any one to one stuff. He enjoyed a drink he sang in pubs and clubs, he was everyone's friend, he knew everybody and everybody knew him. He was very strict, hardworking and enjoyed a good drink. I suppose he was a typical post war man's man, the youngest son of thirteen kids. Born and bred in Oldham, with a strong Irish catholic heritage, when he needed to he would lay on a thick Irish accent, especially when he met friends in the street. I think most of the people he associated with were also Irish, or like him pretending to be, I often wondered who was kidding who.

There was one particular occasion I remember very well, it was when I had been involved in what only can be described as bullying incident by today's standards, not something to be proud of. Although at the time we thought it was just a bit of harmless name calling. This particular incident was brought on by one of our friends, *well a kid in our class*, who on arriving at school on a particularly wet day, was carrying his mum's umbrella. He could have been excused this misdemeanour if it had been at least black, a proper man's umbrella, but no this one was white with a floral pink pattern, it actually was his mums. Therefore to a group of thirteen year olds he was branded a poof, *(come on this was the 70's)*, to be honest if you had a coat with a hood which most of us did and you were caught using said hood when it was raining you were also a poof. So to be seen walking to school with your mums flower pattern umbrella above your head, you were without question a poof. As a result of this name calling which went on for weeks after the event, he told his mum he didn't want to go to school anymore. So an angry Mrs Clarke was soon standing on our doorstep explaining in her best Irish accent the circumstances of the crime, to my now fully fluent pretend Irish speaking dad, I remember looking at him thinking *"dad you aren't even Irish"*, this was long before Peter Kay coined the phrase. A few slaps around the head in front of Mrs Clarke cured my name calling and the poof returned to school the next day, without the umbrella.

After my dad's funeral I didn't notice any real change we just seemed to get on with things, I think I just shut it all out. I don't think we had any time off school as I am sure I returned to school the day after the funeral. I just carried on as normal, played out on my bike did my paper round. Christmas came and went, another birthday in January, a year older. Now fifteen my priorities changed, thoughts of leaving school, not mention my developing interest in girls; I had other things to keep me occupied. In addition to this my uncle Albert offered me a weekend job, working with him as a plumbers mate, well sort of. Sometimes I would also take time off school to help him on larger jobs. I think I became the son he always wanted. I suppose for a short time in a way he replaced the father figure in my life. Not only that he paid me for the work I did, some weeks I could make forty quid, which was good money in 1975. The next 18 months seemed to move on pretty quickly before I knew it I had left school and was on a train to Folkestone, about to start what was going to be a long career in the Army.

How Things Can Quickly Change

In that past eighteen months I fell in love, fell out of love, fell in love again, met my future stepdad, and went on a family holiday to Ilfracombe in Devon. My life was in fast forward mode, thinking back now it was as if I was skipping through the trailers of my life's DVD wanting to get to the good bits and get my life started. I couldn't wait to leave home, and by September 1976 I was ready to face the world.

Chapter 19

Taking the Queens Shilling

I left school in May 1976. I wasn't quite sure what I really wanted to do, what 16 year does? Working with my uncle was OK, but I needed a proper job as I was keen to start making money. Our Mick who left school just two years before me was working as a welder at a small firm in Oldham Town centre just off George Street. They made ornamental gates, telephone and plant stands which were then coated in white plastic, they were quite popular in the seventies. I remember he made one for my mum, although we didn't even have a phone at the time. I went to see him one Monday morning to find out more about his job with a view to doing something similar. It was a small dark workshop just a couple of blokes welding and bending metal rods into scroll shapes and then coating them in a powder which was then fired to give it that plastic coating. To be honest I didn't find it that exciting.

Later that afternoon I found myself looking in the window of the Army Careers office, it was just around the corner from where he worked. This seemed much more exciting than working in a welding shop. To this day I don't know why but I just walked in and asked if I could join, before I knew it I was filling in forms, and was given one which my mum had to sign. I took it home, got her to sign it and took it back the next day. The guy in uniform then handed me a large pink piece of paper which he said was a travel warrant from Oldham to Harrogate in Yorkshire, plus a set of instructions on how to get there, he then told me to be at the train station at Oldham Mumps on Friday at 9.00am. It was Friday before I knew it, and I arrived in Harrogate with over a hundred other kids from all over the Northwest. There were mini busses waiting for us at the station to take us to the barracks. Which at the time was one of the many Army Selection Centres, where kids between the ages of 16 and 17 underwent a number of tests to see what arm of service they were most suited to. Although I don't think I did that well at school I passed all the necessary tests. I remember at one point I was asked what would like to do in the Army, I think I said that I wanted to jump out of helicopters. I had no idea what regiment or corps I would be joining. On Sunday afternoon I was told that I would be enlisted in the Army in September, starting my training at the Junior Leaders Battalion in Folkestone Kent. That was it... I was in... I travelled home feeing quite proud of myself, not everyone was selected, there were some kids crying on the train. For the first time in my life I felt that I had achieved something. I was through to boot camp... literally. I couldn't wait to get home and tell my mum.

It was the long hot summer of 1976. While waiting for my enlistment date I carried on working with Uncle Albert. I found out that plumbing involved more than just fitting bathrooms and unblocking sinks. We carried out a variety of jobs; some involved replacing sewer pipes, not the best job during a heatwave in July and August. At times he was that busy on some jobs he would leave me on my own while he went to estimate another job. On one occasion Albert asked if I had a friend who could go with me to help dig a new manhole and knock down part of an interior wall, while he finished off one of the other jobs. I asked my mate Martin Rafferty who lived just up the road from me and was one of my best friends at the time. He jumped at the chance to make a few extra quid. Little did we know that this day would almost finish us both off? Our main jobs for the day were to knock through a door section within an upstairs back bedroom wall which was being converted into a bathroom at the back of the house. Then we had to dig a manhole in the backyard so we could lay the sewer pipes for the toilet. As soon as we arrived we got on with the task at hand, it was hot and dusty as we both removed the existing plaster to reveal the brickwork underneath. Albert had already marked out the section we had to remove so there was no danger that two sixteen year olds kids would knock down the wrong wall. At times the dust from the plaster was unbearable so we opened the back window which overlooked the yard. It was an old wooden sash window which didn't open evenly, back then the windows operated on an internal pulley system consisting of two large weights inside the cavity wall which helped to control this upward and downward movement, if the rope on the pulley was old or the pulley wheels were rusty they would need a little more persuasions and this was one of those windows that needed to be coaxed but I managed to get it open.

The dust soon cleared and we soon knocked through to the front bedroom and our doorway was complete. The lady of the house brought us some cold lemonade and congratulated us on what we had done so far. She was a middle aged woman with speech impediment when she spoke it was difficult to understand her as she talked down her nose at first I thought she was deaf, she wasn't she was just very nasally. We drank our lemonade thanked Mrs homeowner and moved downstairs to get on with our next task.

We then got started on the manhole, we removed the necessary flags and started digging, as soon as we got down a couple of feet it started raining, it was still hot so we just carried on digging. I could hear Mrs Homeowner shouting something from the upstairs window I had opened earlier. She was trying to tell us that the Plasterboard under the window was getting wet, before I could finish telling her to leave the window it's a little tricky… I'll do it in a minute love, there was an almighty crash I instinctively ran toward the back door Martin ran towards the back gate. The full window had fallen out as she pushed down hard on it to close it. The full pane of glass smashed on the mound of earth we had dug out of the hole and naturally went everywhere most of which went forward in Martins direction. I heard Martin let out a small scream as a large piece of glass stuck in his back just below his kidney. Mrs Homeowner was hysterical and immediately phoned an ambulance. Martin pulled the piece of glass out of his back it wasn't as bad as we first thought but he would need stitches. I held a towel on the wound until the ambulance came. I'm not sure what she said on the phone but it arrived pretty dam quick. Before I knew it I was standing in the backyard on my own surrounded by broken glass and bits of wood. All I could think about was what Uncle Albert was going to say when he got back. I had just finished cleaning up when he arrived back, he came through the back gate, saw me standing alone and said where's your mate? I looked up at the window he looked at me, back at the window, he could see the glass and wood I had put in a neat pile next to the bin. I just looked at him and said an ambulance has taken him to casualty, and tried to explain what Mrs Homeowner had done. I found myself trying to mimic her speech impediment as I told him how it all happened, trying desperately to add humour and defuse the serious situation he could now be facing. Fortunately this was long before the compensation culture we now live in.

That night we went to Martins house to see how he was, he showed us the scar, he did have a couple of stitches, and it could have been a lot more serious if we hadn't moved like shit off a shovel when we heard the crash. Albert just said "glad you are alright lad", handed him £20.00 and said "here you are lad get yourself a new T Shirt" and we left. His mum and dad never batted an eyelid. I never saw Martin again after that.

Chapter 20

Leaving Home

The enlistment day finally came, it was Tuesday the 14th of September 1976 when I walked down Redgrave Street carrying my big heavy suitcase to the bus stop outside the Farmers Boy Pub on Huddersfield Road to catch the bus to Manchester. I sat on the bus alone reading through the instructions on how to get to Folkestone. I didn't even know how far it was, I just knew that I had to get to London Euston, get the underground to Waterloo Station and then catch another train to Folkestone. When I arrived at Manchester Piccadilly Station there seemed to be hundreds of kids, parents, proud mums and dads family members, all there to wave off their little boy soldiers. I felt quite alone despite the number of people there, there was no one there to wave me off. My attention was soon drawn to the two men in uniform from the Army careers office ticking our names off a list and making sure we had our tickets for the train and the underground.

The time came to board the train I dragged my heavy suitcase down the platform to the train. I was one of the first on as I rushed past all the kids hugging their mums and dads, brothers and sisters aunties and uncles, friends and neighbours'. I found a seat by the window, at one point I think I just waved at some random people not to feel totally left out and alone, they actually waved back which made me feel a little better. As the train pulled away I looked around the carriage, it was like a scene from Harry Potter, just kids everywhere, I am sure one kid had an owl. The regular London commuters must have wished they had paid the extra fair for first class that morning, instead of having to endure a journey with overexcited teenage lads. The first stop was at Crew station and more lads got on, more mums and dads waving on the platform, when we then pulled into Birmingham New Street Station there was a bigger crowd, had we gone back in time and National Service was once again compulsory, was war declared? Obviously not, but we later found out that we were part of one of the biggest intakes in the Army since the Second World War.

When we all finally arrived in London we all scuttled around like ants trying to find the entrance to the ant hill. Understandably this was the first time many of us had ventured this far on our own, I'm not sure who we were following but before I knew it I was squashed trapped and squeezed into a carriage on the London Underground. I just hoped and prayed I was on the Northern Line, the black one on the map, the one I had memorised the sequence of stops from my instructions. I felt a little more at ease when we soon arrived at Warren Street, I then saw the map above the door, Goodge Street, Tottenham Court Road, Leicester Square, Charing Cross, Embankment and finally Waterloo, I was on the right train. We all poured out onto the platform and waited for the next train to Folkestone Central. It was yet another hour and forty minutes journey before we finally arrived, waiting for us was a fleet of minibuses ready to ferry us to the camp on the hill. Sir John Moore Barracks home of The Infantry Junior Leaders Battalion (IJLB) in Shorncliffe, Cheriton. On arrival it wasn't long before we were all processed and in uniform, well I say uniform; we were all dressed in green army coveralls and black plimsolls. We looked like juvenile delinquents at a correction centre. I remember sitting next to this kid in the gym as we waited to collect the rest of our uniform. I had not spoken to anyone all day, there were very few words exchanged by anyone to be honest, I think we were all in shock. As we sat there waiting to be called forward, he turned to me and said "where you from?" Oldham, I'm from Oldham, came the reply from this kid who was similar in height and build to me but had a Jimmy Cagney look about him, he said his name was Cecil, fuck off your joking, yeh I am, it's John Dean, but I am from Oldham, honest, I live in Springhead, well I think it's Cecil from now on mate, I'm Mark Mooney.

We were amongst the last to get our kit, which we crammed into a large army issue suitcase and a long green kitbag as we moved down a long line of tables. We were issued two of everything apart from socks we got four pairs of them, a month's supply for most 16 year olds. When it came to the combat jackets we were handed one that was the right size and one that was huge, far too big for my 36 inch chest, I held it up in front of me by the shoulders and it caused an eclipse, I think this is too big Colour Sergeant? "You'll grow into that one lad... Next!" I think he said that to all of us, 23 years later I was still trying to grow into mine. Today it's in the attic providing loft insulation.

After the kit issue we were split into groups outside, which we later realised were our Companies and Platoons. We were then told that we were all now members of

Alberhera Company and our Barracks and Accommodation was over there… as this sergeant pointed to some older red brick buildings we could see in the distance. As if in unison we looked at the smart new accommodation blocks behind us with a sigh of disappointment, in some way similar to the way contestants do on I'm a celebrity get me out of here, when they discover that they are going to the shitty camp. So with a suitcase in one hand and a kit bag over our shoulder we took the long walk to Napier Barracks, our home for the next 11 months. This would be the last time we ever walked anywhere again. The only time you were allowed to walk was when retuning from meals. It was a long walk to the barrack blocks with the rough surface of the suitcase constantly rubbing on the side of your leg as we attempted to march with a kit bag slung over the opposite shoulder. There were about two hundred of us in this long procession that strung out as we all tried desperately to keep up. When we finally arrived on the parade square of the camp, once again our names were called as we now grouped into sections of ten and platoons of forty. We were then shown to our individual blocks each consisting of two large rooms with double metal bunk beds down both sides, each bunk separated by two metal lockers, the two rooms separated by washrooms, showers and toilets. The first thing we all noticed was the highly polished floors, these were like glass despite being wooden; the toilet and washroom floor section was made up of gleaming red tiles, all the taps and copper pipes gleamed in the late afternoon sun that shone through the windows. We could see opened tins of orange coloured floor wax… And what looked like broom handles with blocks of heavy metal at the base. We got to know these very well over the coming months. These were known in the trade as Bumpers, used to give the floors their highly polished appearance, by constantly pushing them backwards and forwards over the surface of the floor. It wasn't long before we became masters of the craft; the phrase "wax on wax off" was one we were familiar with long before Mr Meagi coined the phrase in the 1980's film classic the Karate Kid. (*Note from author you will see lots of film references in this book*).

I ended up sharing a bunk with my new friend Cecil as we all filed into the room two at a time. After placing our army suitcases and kit bags on our beds we were once again summoned outside to be given a quick tour of this small barracks, the tour finished at the cookhouse where we now had our evening meal, after which we were told to collect our own suitcases and baggage which were now in neat rows on the parade square. We returned to our rooms to finally unpack and get acquainted with our new surroundings. That evening we were also introduced to our platoon sergeants and two guys who were former Junior Soldiers from the previous intake who assisted with showing us the basics of life as a boy soldier.

First we were shown how to iron our kit and fold our clothing, and how to lay it out in our steel lockers, everything had its place which had to be meticulously placed in the locker. We soon all started to realise that life as we once knew it had changed forever. I was so pleased that the time I spent learning to iron clothes while stuck at home with my mum during the times when I was off school with asthma gave me a head start on many of them.

It was quite evident that some of these kids had never even plugged an Iron in let alone use one. Some kids were almost in tears because they couldn't iron a shirt and this was just the first day. That first night it was lights out at 10.30pm but there was still some kids desperately trying to iron and fold the khaki KF shirts we had been issued earlier that day. It was a long night for some; you could hear a few of them crying it was like a scene from the Shawshank Redemption, (*"told you, another film reference"*).

Morning came early at 6.00am, our two trained soldiers arrived to guide us through the initial morning routine which included washing and shaving, this was compulsory although at sixteen very few of us needed to shave, nevertheless we still had to go through the motions of having a wet shave, again a new experience for most of us.

By the end of the first week we all naturally formed our own little groups and lifetime friendships were born. This was completely different to the friendships forged at school, although we were still only kids you soon realise that the guys you team up with are the ones you will rely on. It's a little difficult to explain, but I suppose you start to learn the true meaning of trust. You learn to identify the type of guys you want to be watching your back when the time comes. Understandably during that first eleven months it was very unlikely you would be in a life and death experience, but there were times when you found yourself on a mountain either holding on to a length of rope or looking up at the guy holding on to you. Or when you are on a rifle range or a live firing exercise with live ammunition, real bullets! With other guys to the left and right of you, that element of trust couldn't be more important, that's the kind of friendship I mean.

Our platoon was a mixture of kids from all over the UK, it's funny that today we are all familiar with regional accents. Most kids before they even think about leaving school will know the difference between a Geordie, Brummies' or Cockney accent. For us it was strange at first to hear a broad Geordie accent, "ow man where yow from marra? what the fuck did he just say" was a common reply during the first few weeks. Most of us had never stepped out of our home towns until now. We had a right old mix of regional accents in our platoon, Scousers, Mancs, Boltonains, Brummies, Cockneys, Geordies, not to mention an Irishman, Welshman and a Jock, who walked into the room just for the comedy effect. It was weeks before any of us knew what the other was saying.

We all learnt quite a lot during those eleven months of training; although there were times when we did not fully understand what it was they were trying to teach us especially why you have to "get on the bus, then get off the bus". This soon became a common term for anything we had to do more than once and a phrase almost all soldiers will be familiar with. As it was very rare that anything you did wouldn't have to be done again, however you eventually learn that what really matters is attention to detail, if something wasn't right it was done again. Although these lessons can come in many forms, for example, something as trivial as your boot laces being twisted during a morning inspection, was considered a criminal offence and warranted at least twenty press ups, or a run around the drill square with your rifle above your head.

Army training establishments often got a bad press, as conditioning was often misconstrued as bullying. It is actually quite difficult to simulate the environments you are likely to be faced with during an operational environment, and understandably as individuals we are all different. Sadly some people are just not cut out for a life in the armed forces. So I suppose the only way to test the resolve of soldiers is to put them under real physical and mental pressure, quite literally separating the men from the boys. Every old soldier will say that it wasn't like that when I was a lad; we had it much harder than you lot. Although we had long past the tough no nonsense regime of National Service when I joined, I believe the backend of the seventies was still a time when the Army still followed that strict less tolerant routine of how army discipline, training and conditioning was implemented.

Throughout my career I witnessed the changes in attitude toward training methods and the way the softly, softly approach started to creep in. In the mid to late eighties there were a number of programmes on TV that showed life in the barracks of some of the training establishments, which only seemed to focus on what they described as bullying. Because of this many new Commanding Officers of these establishments became a little paranoid, training Corporals and Sergeants were sacked left right and centre, some deservedly and some not, simply victims of circumstance and before we knew it the ball was firmly in the court of the soldier being trained. The same way kids in the classroom seem to have the upper hand over the teachers today, that control over discipline is lost forever. I am not saying that the softly, softly approach is wrong; it's a fine balance of both. Although it's funny that we often comment on how brave the soldiers were during the First and Second World War, and how hard it must have been for them and how ever did they cope? The truth is they had no choice they just got on with it. If we continue to question every method on why things are done a particular way we simply end up where we are now, we create a blame culture, nothing is ever our fault, mistakes we make are always someone else's problem. I knew that all the problems I faced during those recent dark periods in my life were all created by me, there was no one else to blame but me.

Perhaps some of the methods used to teach me discipline may have been wrong, but we never complained we accepted it, the same way many of us will say that smacking never did us any harm when we were kids. I thoroughly enjoyed my time at IJLB.

Chapter 21

Passing Out

As the weeks progressed our platoons of forty were now dwindling fast as some kids realised that the Army was not for them or they simply did not cut the mustard. The bunk beds soon became single bunks and the barrack rooms were far less cramped as we approached our final passing out parade, before we joined our regiments and regular battalions.

Over the course of those eleven months I was completely re-educated, quite literally, at times we did actually go back to school, and there was an education bock in the newer part of the camp. In addition to the training you would naturally associate with becoming a professional Infantry soldier, fieldcraft, weapons training etc. We also sat English and Maths tests, we also had to choose a hobby which we did once a week. We had an opportunity to pick from a selection of activities which included horse riding, archery and Judo, plus a few more which I can't remember, chess clubs, war gaming and stuff like that I think. Our first choice was horse riding. I'd always fancied myself as a jockey, although I had never been on a horse, Cecil (*new nickname shortened to Cess by this stage*), had ridden before, to be honest it was actually his idea. He said that he heard that there were girls at the stables, there always is. He was right the riding club was run by two women in their late forties, officers' wife's who were very… well let's just say they were scarier than some of the Drill Sergeants, there were some younger girls there but they always left when we all arrived. During our first visit to the stables we didn't even get on a horse, we spent the first session leaning about the horses welfare, cleaning, grooming, shovelling shit (they called it manure), but we knew it was shit, (*I know old gag, sorry*"). We did eventually get on a horse and the first thing that stuck me was how far off the ground you are, horses are big fuckers. The furthest we got in our new found hobby was to the rising trot, laterally bouncing up and down on horseback until your arse is numb. At the end of the third session we both looked at each other and said "fuck it, let's try Archery".

We found that Archery was run by our Platoon Commander so that was only a onetime session; we saw enough of him during the day thank you very much. Judo was our next choice, on arrival at the gym on that first Tuesday session I was immediately issued a judo suit (Judogi), we were taught how to break your fall, how to pull people off balance and the most important thing from my point of view at the time was that little blokes are better at it than the big guys. Over the course of the coming weeks and months Judo was my thing, I loved it, not only that I was actually quite good at it. Unfortunately just a few days before the Junior Leaders Championships I was training with another guy who was a few grades higher, a blue belt, and also in a slightly heavier weight class than me. He was showing me a new throw, which didn't quite go my way. I landed on my shoulder, and he came crashing down on top of me and broke my collarbone. The QMSI (the guy in charge), thought that I had just dislocated my shoulder and said he could reset it, reset what? I could see the bone almost sticking out of my skin, there was no way I was going to let this nutter near me. I was taken to the local hospital and it was confirmed that I had broken my clavicle (collarbone). For the next six weeks my shoulders were strapped back, it was as if I was permanently standing to attention, *"shoulders back lovely boy"*. Despite my injury I was still allowed to attend training... well all the stuff that didn't require crawling about in the undergrowth. If this injury had happened a few weeks later I would have been back squaded, which means doing some of the training all over again resulting in not passing out with all your mates you have just spent the last eleven months with.

It normally takes six to eight weeks for a collarbone to heal, but less than five weeks after my injury I was running about on the ranges firing anti-tank weapons, throwing live grenades', there was no way I was going to miss this. If it had been my right shoulder I had injured there was no way I would have been able to take part in this final training before a major training exercise which was a culmination of all the infantry skills we had learnt over the full training period.

Our final battle camp was at Otterburn close to the Cheviot Hills, a place I became more familiar with as my career progressed. During that first experience of this terrain we soon learned that rapid changes in weather conditions could quite easily turn a situation on its head, even in the summer months. One particular memory was on a night route march when our platoon sergeant got disorientated when the mist descended on us and he made an almost fatal mistake of not trusting his compass, as we almost wandered into an area of a live night firing exercise (*real bullets*), of another unit. This was my first experience of real fear as we could hear the rounds whistling over our heads as we scrambled over rocks to the safety of dead ground. It took us all night to get back to camp.

We spent two weeks at Otterburn, during that month in July, I enjoyed every day of this final exercise although at times it seemed like hard work, especially when we had to dig our first battle trench. Naturally I was paired up with my sparring partner Cess. We got through two picks, broke three shovels, smashed through rocks like prisoners on a chain gang, but managed to get to stage one before first light, just before being attacked by the enemy. Fortunately Stage one for two short arses from Oldham is a trench depth of just four feet, which was chest height for us. At the end of a dawn attack the exercise scenario is always very similar; in fact almost every Infantry exercise follows the same pattern. You walk for miles over difficult terrain, with all your kit you meet small pockets of resistance along the way, you then dig in, and you defend that ground for a few days. Wait for the enemy to attack you, which is always at dawn. You do what's known in military terms as a tactical withdrawal, re-group attack the enemy and by lunch time you hear the words that everyone loves to hear… END EX! END EX! You then go back and fill in all the holes you spent all that time digging. Marvellous eh (*sarcastic tone…*)

With all the infantry skills stuff done our attention was now focused on our final passing out parade. Now it was all about looking smart polishing boots marching in straight lines with Rifles and Bayonets fixed, drums beating bands playing. Although the numbers dwindled during the course of those eleven months this was still one of the biggest intakes in the Army for quite some time. The final parade took weeks of preparation, by the end of which we were all bursting with pride. We were told that all our parents and families would be there. To be honest I didn't think my mum was going to be there, Folkestone was a long a long way from Kansas Toto, would Gerald's old yellow Ford Cortina make it that far?

The day before the parade my platoon commander handed me a piece of paper with an address, to my surprise it was for a campsite my mum and Gerald where staying at just outside Folkestone called the Little Switzerland Caravan and camping site. They had been to the barracks earlier that day to see if they could find me. I asked my two best mates if they wanted to come with me, they jumped at the chance, as it was the perfect excuse to get out of camp for a few hours. The three of us jumped in a taxi, not quite sure where we were going as I handed the address to the driver. About thirty minutes later we arrived at this site on top of the cliffs near Dover. I told my mates to look out for a bright yellow Ford Cortina, "what that one over there with the bonnet up?" they said in unison. Understandably it stuck out like the preferable sore thumb. My mum was so pleased to see me, as I introduced my friends John Dean (Cess) and Tony Bibby a lad from Bolton. While we were there two young women turned up a few minutes after we arrived, one was Gerald's daughter (Dilys) and her friend Speedy, and ironically they were both in the WRAC and serving at the same camp as drivers. I had been at the camp for almost a year and never knew that my stepsister was serving at the same camp, although she wasn't yet officially my stepsister at the time.

We spent an hour with them all before we had to get back to camp, my mum said they had a bit of a nightmare of a journey and broke down a few times on route. This was nothing new, it was simply par for the course were Gerald was concerned, he was never happier unless he was under the bonnet of a car. He was actually tightening the fan belt when we arrived.

When we left he gave us a lift back down the hill and dropped us off in Folkestone, we then jumped back in a taxi went back to camp to put the final touches to our best kit for the parade the next day. It's funny I never knew why he didn't take us all the way back to camp.

The Passing Out Parade was a proud moment for us all as we marched on to the Drill square for the final time. Thinking back I remember that feeling of achievement, a similar feeling to the way I felt when I crossed the line on the Mall during the London Marathon, although many have done it before you and with you on the day, it's a sense of personal pride that only you can feel at the time, I was so pleased with myself.

Chapter 22

The Bermuda Triangle

After the passing out parade we spent a few more days in camp handing back kit and equipment, before we went on leave. We were also told which Battalions we would be joining. Prior to being given this news I assumed I would be joining the 3rd Battalion The Royal Regiment of Fusiliers with all my fellow Mancs and Lancashire mates, however the Platoon commander seemed to take great pleasure in announcing that Mooney and Dean were joining the 1st Battalion along with all the Geordies in the platoon. Not that there is anything wrong with Geordies it just seemed a little strange that two lads from Oldham where posted to the Battalion that had strong links to the former Regiment of The Northumberland Fusiliers and not the one with a stronger Lancashire history. I suppose it was all about numbers as we were simply split down the middle, sending an equal number of new recruits to the three existing battalions', or was it fate?

After that short break of leave which seemed to be over in a flash. I found myself once again standing on a platform in Manchester with my almost brand new Army suitcase and Kit Bag over my shoulder, on my way to Oakington Barracks in Cambridge. Even without the suitcase and kit bag it was easy to spot soldiers returning from leave, the short hair was a big give away in the late seventies. It wasn't long before I was approached by two lads, who seem to make a beeline for me as soon as I put my bags down.

In normal circumstances I would be crapping myself, but as I said the short hair was a dead giveaway and it was quite clear these two were either squaddies or plain clothes police offices. Not only were they soldiers themselves they were also members of the same battalion and on their way to Cambridge. They too had been on leave after returning from a training exercise in Kenya, which they took great pleasure in telling me all about for the next five hours.

One of these lads was from Rochdale a guy named Pete Gallimore the other lad Phil Barker was from Oldham. They also told me what to expect when I got there and that life in the battalion is a lot slower than in training, they said that most of the time you sit around doing nothing, and explained that the battalion was currently on Spearhead, at the time I thought this was just another Kenya reference but later discovered that Spearhead meant that no matter where there was trouble in the world our unit would be the first to go. They also said that next week we are going on a Battalion Exercise in Otterburn (*shit I'd just come from there*).

Sadly both Phil and Pete were later killed in Northern Ireland, Phil was killed at a checkpoint in Belfast during my first tour in 1980 to 81, he was shot in the head at point blank range on the 25th January 1981 aged just 25. Pete was killed as a result of a car bomb in May 1984 while on a fishing trip in Enniskillen, this was during a two year tour when I was then working alongside the intelligence services, but more on that later. Two others Tommy Agar and Bob Hugging died at the scene, another lad named Clive Aldridge survived but lost both his legs. Pete actually survived the initial blast and died in hospital five months later on the 18th October 1984.

When I arrived at Oakington I found that I was in the same Platoon and Company as Pete, 7 Platoon Y company along with and my friend from training, Cess (John Dean), plus a few more new recruits who had arrived from the Queens Division Depot in Bassingbourn. One particular guy who stood out on account of his size was a kid called Jonathan Fairburn a big blonde Geordie bloke, AKA Jaws, and future cell mate of mine, but again more on that later. Before we knew it we were once again digging a trench on Otterburn training area just a few metres from where we were before, the grass had only just started growing back, the problem was I was now digging a trench with Jaws, chest height for him was head height for me. When we returned from Otterburn six weeks later it was back into the routine of sitting around waiting for things to happen, some weekends we did manage to get home. My relationship with Linda was now back on so I was keen to get back for the weekend, but I hated the journey back on Sunday night it just seemed to take forever there were no direct trains to Cambridge unless you went via London so that was out of the question. Some weekends you could get a lift for £15.00, one of the regular drivers and owner of a mini bus was a Pakistani lad from Oldham nicknamed Basha, (*I'm not going to explain that one but remember things were different in the seventies*), unfortunately places were booked in advance and you only managed to get a lift if someone dropped out or was on duty at short notice. The cheapest option to getting home was to thumb a lift; hitchhiking was something many of us did back then. The A1 North was just two miles from camp so we would walk to the services at Bar Hill. At times it became very competitive as we would compete with each other along the route of the A1 North to Ferrybridge where we would join the M62 to Oldham and Manchester. We basically lived for the weekend as camp life became monotonous and repetitive. Although I had only been there for a few months I soon got bored with the routine, until that first weekend in December 1977 when my outlook on the Army changed forever.

All members of Y Company were confined to camp due to it being our turn to act as lead company as part of our Spearhead duties. On Saturday night we were just sat around the barrack room listening to music and trying to tune in one of those all-in-one telly things with a picture the size of a fag packet. The only guy with a proper telly at the time was our section commander "George No Hair" aptly named on the account that he was going bald (real name George O'Hare), imaginative souls us squaddies eh! He had his own bunk at the end of the main room, suddenly he popped his bald head around the door and shouted come and look at this there's something going on in Bermuda. We didn't quite catch the full news story but there was some mention that troops from Belize had been called to assist with some kind of civil disturbance and riots and it was likely that more support would come from standby units in the UK. It wasn't long before we were all thinking the same thing, and before we knew it we were getting issued Tropical Combats and on our way to Brize Norton. Before leaving camp we all rushed to the phones to call our families, the problem I had was that my mum and Linda's mum didn't have a phone at the time the only person who did was Linda's older brother Derek, I called him and just said can you tell Linda to tell my mum that I am going to Bermuda, he said when? Now! I'm not sure if he believed me at the time. When we arrived at Brize Norton there was a film crew waiting for us, it was just crazy, I was still only 17 years old and flying halfway around the world having only been in the battalion less than four months. It was a long 12 hour flight with a brief stop in Canada, we arrived in Bermuda in the early hours of the morning on the 5th of December. When we touched down the realisation started to hit me as I was handed a rifle and a magazine and ten live rounds. The Sergeant Major told me to get on the back of what was an ordinary Luton type van with an open roller shutter at the back. He said stick that magazine on your rifle Mooney lad and jump in the back, while he got in the front with the driver. It's fair to say that I was crapping myself. I had no idea where we were going, most of the other members of the company got on old Bedford trucks which belonged to the Bermuda Defence Regiment. Fortunately it was only a short drive to the camp in Hamilton, south west of the island, in fact everything in Bermuda is a short drive its only about 22 miles long and 2.5 miles wide. Once we settled in we soon got into the routine of guarding the key points (KP's) dotted around the island. These included The Governors' House, The Electric and Lighting Company, The TV and Radio Station and Airport. To be honest it was quite uneventful while we were there, but one kid almost killed himself when he fell about thirty or forty feet off the top of the building at the electric light company (BELCO). One of our tasks was to patrol the grounds at night and the tops of the buildings where naturally good look out points, we had just rotated our shift and were sat in the café section of the building. The room we were in had large high windows and directly opposite was a much taller building with a flat roof, although we could not see the top as we sat there drinking coffee and eating cake at 1am. Suddenly out of the corner of my eye along with a few others we all saw this thing fall past the window and heard what can only be described as a dull thud, "what the fuck was that"? We rushed outside to find this lad Steve Butler a kid from Manchester lying on a small piece of grass, to the left of him were some steps and to the right a small wall. He had just fallen over 30 feet from the top of the building and landed on the only piece of grass in the whole complex, "you lucky bastard Butler", sympathetic squaddies aren't they. It's funny how a serious situation suddenly becomes hilarious. We looked up to see the lad we nicknamed Jaws peering over the edge of the roof above us. "Fuckin hell Jaws as thrown the little fucker off the top", was one assumption that immediately came from our small crowd of onlookers. By the way for the record the ambulance was on its way by this time and first aid was being administered. As a result of the fall he actually smashed his shoulder and right arm and broke a few ribs and spent a few weeks in hospital, we had returned to the UK before he came out. Jaws aptly nicknamed due to his size, and named based on the character from the popular 70's Bond film Moonraker, said Steve was pulling a large concrete bock which had a handle on one side, slowly dragging it to the edge of the roof so he could sit on it. Jaws said I was helping him by pushing the other end. When I looked up I just saw his little feet going over the edge. Well at least he got a free holiday out of it, and the chance to spend Christmas in Bermuda, was another sympathetic comment that came from a mate of his.

When we all returned from Bermuda just before Christmas 1977 we found that the remainder of the battalion had been called to assist with the Fireman's Strike. As soon as we touched down in Brize Norton we were on our way to Colchester for some quick Fire Fighting Training, then on to Bromley in Kent to join other members of the Battalion. Christmas leave was well and truly cancelled that year. This kept us occupied until 12th January 1978 when the strike ended just a week before my 18th Birthday.

Chapter 23

18 Years Old & Engaged To be Married

To be honest I can't remember much of my 18th Birthday I remember going out with my mates on that Wednesday night to the local Cambridge haunts, the Still and Sugarloaf and the Red Cow. Although I can remember waking up the next morning fully clothed and there was a pile of sick around my bed. The strange thing I remember there being sheets of newspaper around my bed, protecting the shiny floor, obviously put down as a precaution by my trusted colleagues. When I woke I was the only one in the room as everyone else was on parade for morning muster. Thank god someone covered for me and said that I had reported sick, which was a slight understatement. I was in bits; this was one of those never again moments which for some reason you quickly forget. Fortunately the rest of the day was just an admin day prior to us all going on a long weekend.

When I went home that weekend Linda and I decided to get engaged we had been together for almost three years on and off. There was no big announcement or party, no buffet, not even a Seventies Disco. I don't even remember getting down on one knee, well not in public. But I think I have made up for it over the years, because I have been on my knees many times since, insert your own thoughts here but not in a 50 shades kind of way.

Our first engagement lasted about seven months and just for the record kids, it was your mother who broke it off. I was serving in Cyprus at the time on a six month UN tour. I'll get back to that in a moment; however prior to the tour I experienced one of my being in the right place at the right time moments. This was during a weekend in February that year, most weekends we would go home but this was one of those occasions when I was on guard duty on Friday night, so going home was not on the cards that weekend.

On Sunday morning I was sat on my bed polishing my boots, there was a few of us in the room cleaning our kit, when the COS (Company Orderly Sergeant), a Lance Corporal named Tommy Agar (*sadly killed along with the others in the car bombing I mentioned earlier*). He came in asking if anyone had a provisional driving licence. "I have it's in my locker" I replied, "pack your kit Marra your off to Leconfield on a driving cadre, the Sergeant Major just asked me to find anyone with a provisional licence to fill a vacant slot, because some soft sod has not made it back in time, and the transport to the station leaves in 45min". You jammy bastard! was the response from the others in the room, my face was brimming with delight, this was a lottery win, at least five numbers and the bonus ball, albeit that the lottery had not been invented yet, it's fair to say that I was much more than pleased.

I need to explain the kudos in being given such a gift as a Driving Cadre so early in your career, especially when I had only been in the battalion for a few months. You're not normally considered for such a sought after course unless

18 Years Old and Engaged to be Married

you had served at least three or four years, so for a sprog to be given this rare opportunity was not the norm. Learning to drive at the MOD's expense was one of those few things that didn't come around too often.

On this occasion the Battalion needed additional qualified drivers for the forthcoming tour in Cyprus. Each Platoon needed at least four Land Rover drivers as part of the commitment on the UN phase, and in the Sovereign Base in Dhekelia.

Along with a group of others I arrived at Leconfield a former RAF camp in Beverley near Hull, its sole purpose was to train drivers, everything from something as small as Mini to Class 1 HGV's, Busses and other large heavy logistic vehicles. On Monday morning we were split into two man groups and introduced to our civilian driving instructors and let loose on the airfield to learn the basics of pulling away, stopping and the fundamentals' of clutch control.

Sections of the airfield had been converted to represent normal roads with working traffic lights, zebra crossings, lollypop ladies, kids and cyclists, (Joking about the lollypop ladies and the kids). We spent a couple of days on the airfield driving a small black mini with duel pedals before we were let loose on the open roads in and around Hull and North East Yorkshire. At times it was like a scene from the Italian Job, (*sorry another film reference*), as we all left the camp at the same time in a convoy of minis.

My instructor was a former BSM (*British School of Motoring*) instructor, now employed by the MOD, a civilian named Norman who was in his late 50's. It was a refreshing change to be taught a skill without someone screaming in your face, thinking back, the best way to describe him was that he was a bit like Norris off Coronation Street, he always had something to talk about. I remember not saying much in return as I was far too busy concentrating on the job of learning to drive.

I past my driving test after about three weeks but not before failing a couple of times. Getting that pass certificate was my first real experience of achievement, since the passing out parade. Although it would be nice to say that I past first time, I suppose failing something a couple of times makes it more of an achievement, that's my excuse and I'm sticking to it...

On return to camp we then needed to transfer our new skills to driving Land Rovers and trailers, which added a whole new concept to reversing. If you have ever tried reversing a trailer I am sure you will know what I mean. The Land Rovers we had back then where quite old and changing gear meant we had to learn the technique of doubling the clutch (double de-clutch), apparently due to there being no synchromesh in the old gearbox of these clapped-out Land Rovers. Why I needed to tell you that I don't know?

Chapter 24
Lizards a Jail Sentence and a Goat Named Ragman

Just a few weeks later I found myself driving troops and dropping them off at the OP's, observation posts, along the borderline, commonly known as the Barrel line or Green Line, or was it the Buffer Zone, that separated the Greek and Turkish sectors, during our operational UN tour in Northern Cyprus as part of UNFICYP (*United Nations Forces in Cyprus*).

These were daily trips along Buffer Zone, following Miles of dusty track marked by blue and white oil barrels, with the occasional markings for mine fields on the Turkish side. Our Platoon of thirty lived in a converted villa, known as Bravo 25, in any normal situation if this could have been a holiday destination, as it would have been a nice place to take a holiday. The view across the border was quite picturesque. Not that I appreciated it at the time.

In addition to the duties of driving I also took my turn in standing on the roof of the villa looking out across the border, logging any troop movement on the Turkish side. Most of the time nothing happened apart from the odd sighting of lizards running up the walls, on the villa adjacent to ours which was occupied by our Company Commander. To be honest nothing ever happened, but we were there just in case the Turks decided to invade the Greek sector, which they had done just less than four years earlier. Our primary role was to report any build-up of troop activity.

At night we would double up, on duty (stag) spending two hours in the box on the roof. Although we were there during the height of the summer, at night it was often very cold, especially during the early hours of the morning. The night time duty was staggered which meant that during your two hour duty each hour would be spent with a different person. Allow me to explain how this works, not to insult your intelligence, but I need to put in perspective what happened next.

After last light which was normally between the hours of 1900hrs to 2000hrs (7pm to 8pm), the guy who started his two hour duty at 6pm would be joined by another guy at 7pm, the guy who had started at 6pm would be replaced by the another guy who was starting his duty at 8pm. And so it when on throughout the hours of darkness. The significance of this is that during your second hour you could then take turns in relaxing for a few minutes. On occasion you could also grab a quick nap while the other guy continued to observe the darkness for any signs of movement/invasion of Turkish troops.

After two or three weeks into the tour the routine was well established. On one particular day I found myself driving all day due to someone being off sick, this meant that I was driving various details/duties well into the night. My first stint in the box on the roof was at 2am, having had very little sleep prior to this duty meant I was starting to feel the effects of the working day during my second hour, it's fair to say that I was knackered. At 3am the changeover took place and I was allowed to relax for a while. The guy who joined me was my good friend Jaws. If you recall this was the same guy who was on the roof in Bermuda when the guy fell off. Jaws was also a fellow member of the boxing team, and soon to be my cell mate.

That evening there was quite a breeze which caused the door on the OP (the box) to continually bang, so we tied the handle to the door frame to secure it. During the final hour of my duty I sat on the floor to grab a few minutes and told Jaws to give me a kick before the changeover. This was something almost everyone did during what was known as the dead man stag. The next thing I remember was the door of the OP being kicked in by the Guard Commander who was supervising the final changeover from 4am to 6am. He found us both flaked out on the floor, Jaws had also decided to take a nap. Sleeping on duty was a serious offence, we were well and truly fucked.

The Guard Commander told the platoon Sergeant, who over breakfast mentioned it to the Platoon Commander. He naturally mentioned it to the Company Commander who always visited us on a daily basis as we were his closest neighbours. Understandably we were both summoned after breakfast and found ourselves on Company Commanders Orders by 9am. Those familiar with the way military law works, will know that commanding offers have limited powers relating to the seriousness of the crime. He remanded us for CO's Orders, this normally takes a few days sometimes weeks depending on the situation. To our astonishment we found ourselves in front of the CO before midday; subsequently resulting in us both serving 28 days detention in the cells at St David's Camp. This was a massive shock to the system; anyone who has served time in any military jail will know that it's most definitely hard labour. The first week was hard to adjust to, especially the heat, we were the only residents in the cells at the time and the Provost Staff certainly got a kick out of bouncing us around the camp performing a number of daily tasks. We were constantly busy doing some shitty job, often referred to as fatigues' everything from washing an endless mountain of pots and greasy pans in the various mess halls around the camp, peeling spuds, painting white stones, white washing walls. One day I almost went blind due to the sun reflecting off the white paint.

The problem our platoon faced, was that they were two men down, however we found ourselves being signed out at night so we could carry out a duty back at the OP. Basically anyone could sign us out for any purpose or some shitty job they couldn't find anyone else to do. As long as they signed what was known as a "Live Body Receipt" to be more precise this was a book which was often checked by the orderly officer as part of his routine checks. It's the orderly officers' duty to check the welfare of soldiers under sentence. So when they visit the guardroom and request to see the prisoners understandably the provost staff have to account for the whereabouts of the soldiers under sentence. The book is used to prove our whereabouts, and that you were alive when you were signed out, (*everything is signed for in the army*). There were books for everything including one for showers, cigarettes, if I recall we were allowed just three cigarettes per day, which we signed for, one after each mealtime. This was pretty crap if you were a twenty a day man, as I was at the time, in fact almost all of us smoked back in the 70's.

When we were present at the time of the orderly officers inspection we would stand to attention outside our cell and repeat the lines we had rehearsed, *"24433098 Fusilier Mooney, serving 28 days detention for sleeping on duty, no requests or complaints sir!"* It's not what I wanted to say, because like all prisoners I was innocent. After all it was this big dozy Geordie fucker next to me that fell asleep sir, I was just resting my eyes, and now after doing all these shitty jobs in camp we still have to go back to the OP and stag on, (*but I never actually said that*).

During one particular visit back to the OP it was one of the lads 25th Birthday, he was a popular likable character, named Paddy and one of the oldest members of the platoon. I asked the platoon sergeant if I could make him a cake, he agreed and said if its shit I will get the CO to extend your sentence you little tosser.

The time I spent as a kid watching my mum make something out of nothing came in handy. I searched the kitchen for all the ingredients I needed. I made the cake and even managed to create icing which I piped and decorated the cake like a star baker on a popular TV show. The platoon commander Mr Hollywood (*not his real name*), was impressed with my handy work, he was even more pleased when he found out that I could also make pancakes; which he wanted for supper almost every night after I became Star Baker!

Prior to the tour in addition to the training for extra drivers, platoons also needed chefs, to allow us to be more self-sufficient. So prior to the deployment to Cyprus members of the platoon could volunteer for a crash course in food hygiene and learn the basics of cooking. Although this was not a course I attended due to being away driving instead. I found out that I was much better at creating culinary delights than the guy currently assigned to the job.

My previous 28 day sentence was reduced to 18 days due to good behaviour, and I returned to the OP employed as the platoon chef. A job I revelled in, although it was quite challenging cooking for 30 hungry blokes and a goat. The goat by the way was a gift from the local villagers, which we were supposed to kill and eat, but we decided to keep it as a pet and a kind of mascot, which was named Ragman. Why Ragman? Quite simply this was the name used by the platoon sergeant, if anyone was looking particularly scruffy on parade the phrase you look like a "Ragman's Donkey" was quite commonly used, which was shortened to simply Ragman, as he pointed to you while conducting his inspection. When the goat was first presented to us it looked scruffy and un-kept, it was without doubt a Ragman!

I enjoyed my time as the platoon chef as this allowed me some level of independence, although I wasn't aware of it at the time, looking back now I can see that this first taste of individualism was something I was much more comfortable with. Although I also class myself as a team player, who works well with others, well that's what it said on my many reports, nonetheless if the opportunity arises were I can work independently I will jump at the chance.

Every week I would jump in a Land Rover and drive to the main kitchen at St David's Camp to collect the supplies for the coming week. My time in jail meant that my previous stints working in the main kitchen and offers mess allowed me to see the meals the bigger kitchens where producing. I was also now entering the kitchen in the capacity as a chef (*well sort of*). As I was dressed in cooks' whites and I now earned a little more respect from the master chef, he seemed to like my enthusiasm, especially when I handed him my list of ingredients. Although most of the dishes we prepared included chicken, I did my best to produce a variety of chicken dishes, curries, pies and salads. Not forgetting my famous pancakes which now had a drizzle of maple syrup and ice cream, which no doubt pleased the platoon commander.

Chapter 25

Quite Simply Dear John It's Over

The first three months of our Cyprus tour passed pretty quickly and before we knew it, it was time to leave our villa and take the trip south to the second phase of this posting. We arrived at the Sovereign Base at Dhekelia Garrison, sadly Ragman did not join us and was probably a guest at the offers mess. Mmmm Kleftiko tasty…

The final three months of the tour were much more enjoyable, although we still had a number of operational commitments at the Sovereign Base. Nevertheless there was more time for water sports and an opportunity to enjoy the fantastic weather associated with the height of the summer in Cyprus. Unfortunately the separation from my fiancé was starting to take its toll.

Throughout the tour we continued to write to each other, to be honest I wrote almost every day. After all we were engaged and planning our wedding. Linda kept me up-to-date with the plans and things seemed to be going smoothly. Getting mail from home was something we all looked forward to, and receiving letters from family, friends and loved ones, girlfriends, was always a real morale booster. Having said that, the letters from Linda started to dwindle, until one day that letter I was never expecting to arrive, arrived. It was all over, the long periods of separation had taken effect. It's fair to say that I was gutted, this was my first experience of rejection, something almost all of us will go through at some time in our lives. I remember sitting on a large rock looking out to sea watching the sunset on what was a warm perfect July summer evening. There was going to be no wedding no honeymoon, my day was far from perfect, my heart was well and truly broken. I did what almost all soldiers did in those circumstances, I went to the NAAFI and got pissed. The next day I felt shit, not because of the hangover, that ache in my stomach was something else. My head was all over the place, although it was now almost 37 years ago, at the time of writing this chapter, I can still remember how I felt. Unfortunately I am not a professional creative writer so I am limited to my own interpretation, bit ask any eighteen year old how he feels after he has been dumped by his first true love and he will probably say the same thing, "he feels shit". In time you get over it, although that time goes VERY slowly.

During almost all deployments there was always time for some R&R, Rest and Recuperation. Sometimes this is done in platoon or company groups, on this occasion only two or three lads from each platoon would be off at the same time, due to operational commitments. I took my R&R with a Geordie lad called Wes Armstrong, and now that the wedding was off I decided to spend the money I had saved during the earlier part of the tour. One advantage of being on an operational tour is that quite often there is very little to spend your money on. So we both made the most of the money we both had and decided to find the best five star hotel in Larnaca or was it Limassol? We simply asked a Taxi driver to take us to the best hotel he knew. We checked in a to what was a luxury hotel, used by all the officers, which was probably owned to his brother. We spent the whole time drinking brandy sours, lying about in the sun topping up the tan. That week seemed to pass very quickly. To be honest I don't remember much, I think most of the time I was thinking about Linda and the honeymoon that never was. This was the second time we had broken up so I thought this was definitely the end for us.

When the tour was over we returned to Oakington Barracks in Cambridge at the end of September 1978. We went on leave shortly after. When I arrived home my mum said there was a letter for me. To my surprise it was from Linda, she said she would like to meet up and talk things over. She asked if I could meet her from work. It had been over seven months since we had seen each other, I had butterflies in my stomach as I jumped on the bus to meet her. To be honest I don't think she was expecting me to turn up. I waited outside the large mill complex where she worked as a milliner at Failsworth Hats. This was long before mobile phones and texting so there was no way she was going to know I was going to be there. I stood at the entrance watching the workers leave the mill. At first I didn't recognise her, there was something different about her. She looked great, her hair was longer and now in a shaggy perm, she gave me the biggest smile I have ever seen. Although there was no Heathcliff moment, we did not rush into each other's arms or anything like that, we simply held hands and walked to the bus stop. We sat on the bus and both knew that we were just meant to be, we decided to give it another go. After that short break of leave I returned to barracks, once again I was living for the weekend and got home when I could. Now that I had my driving licence, on occasion I would hire a car and sell spaces to other lads who lived in Oldham, the money didn't cover the cost of the hire but it more than paid for the petrol which was about 78p per gallon back then, not quite sure why that's of any significance?

The remaining months of 1978 were quite boring, barrack room life/routine gets to you after a while, then came the Ambulance strike which broke the monotony and once again we found ourselves on standby. In late January 1979 we received confirmation of our posting to Germany, which was for the obligatory four years. Once again I found myself on another driving course, this was for tracked vehicles, in particular the old 432 APC (Armoured Personal Carrier). Over 15 tonnes of raw power, the mechanised infantries' very own mobile home. I soon learned that the best seat was indeed the driver's seat especially when there are eight men with all there kit crammed into the back. We deployed to Germany in the summer of 1979, just a couple of weeks after getting married to Linda. We spent the first few months of married life apart, (*no change there then*), while I concentrated on reaching the first rung of the promotion ladder. It's fair to say that Linda was very supportive throughout my career and simply let me get on with it. (*Did I mention that*)?

I passed the NOC's Cadre and gained my first stripe, I was now an Infantry Lance Corporal, a section 2IC, the second in command of eight men. This is not the best job in the world, as it's not long before you learn that shit travels downhill and stops at you. No doubt the same as it is at any level of junior management; however the money was a little better. By the end of October Linda was ready to join me in Germany, now six months pregnant and expecting our first born. We moved into our first home together, a two bedroom flat on the outskirts of Minden. A typical army married quarter with all the standard furnishings, all listed on an inventory, and laid out in true military fashion, ready to be counted and ticked off during what was known as the March in process. All the things we dreamed about were now starting to come true, but I don't remember dreaming about the green camouflage furniture and the service issue four shelf bookcase that occupied the living room. Despite our previous setbacks and short breaks in our relationship, I suppose we always knew we would be together.

Chapter 26
New Baby, New Car
and a Mountain of Debt

Before we knew it we were spending our first Christmas together, although we were away from family and friends back home, Linda seemed to settle to life as an army wife pretty quickly, if she didn't she did not let on. The advantage of living in a service community is that we are all in the same boat, *so to speak*. The wives all face the same challenges and the support network was great as there was always someone there to offer a helping hand, be it advice, a friendly chat or a shoulder to cry on. The families' office and wives' guild provided the foundation of this support. Creating a community spirit that seems to be lacking in today's society was something special. Today we all seem to get on with our own life's and very rarely speak to anyone beyond our immediate neighbours, if at all.

Our first Christmas was great, there is something about being in Germany at Christmas, and anyone who's been there will know what I mean, it just smells like Christmas. Little did we know that being together at Christmas was a very rare opportunity. During my 23 years' service we can count on one hand the times we spent Christmas together as a family, due to various operational commitments. That first Christmas came and went and before we knew we were sitting in an ambulance on our way to the British Military Hospital at Rinteln. Linda went into labour just before midnight on the 28th February. I was about to become a dad, it was a long wait, our little boy Mark was finally born at 13.15 on the 29th February 1980, a leap year baby. He certainly took his time, Linda was in labour for over 13hrs, a forceps delivery, and at times it seemed a little touch and go. She did a fantastic job, understandably childbirth is something us men cannot imagine. However when you witness a forceps delivery especially if you are at the business end, you get a perspective of how difficult and how much pain our beautiful wives go though... Although I distinctly remember Linda telling me never again as her fingernails sunk into the flesh of my hand (*we both needed stiches that day*). It would be almost eight years before she went through it all over again, and a third time seven years later. (*I was away a lot*).

We were now a family, my original plan was to serve just 3 years in the Army, but life in Germany was quite good. So I decided to sign on for six years. Like almost everyone who was serving in Germany at the time, owning and driving a brand new car was a must. So it wasn't long before I was also signing a NAFFI hire purchase agreement for a brand new Silver Talbot Horizon, (*the small family car of the years in 1980 allegedly*). It was going to take me five years to pay for it. At the time I remember there was about half a dozen of us who fell for the same spiel from a slick salesman. We all travelled to Paris on the train to collect our shiny new cars from the main Peugeot dealerships in France. It was a long 12 hour journey, as I shared a carriage with a bunch of German student hippy types, on their way to a festival, who insisted on singing folk songs all the way there.

New Baby, New Car and a Mountain of Debt

The long journey home in my shiny new car was something else, by this stage I had been driving for almost three years, including 15 tonnes of APC. So I classed myself as a confident/competent driver, but nothing could have prepared me for the chaos of driving though the centre of Paris in a brand new car. It was as if all of Paris was saying... *"Look there's another brit in a new French car, get le-twat"*... pardon my French. They came at me from all directions. It took me hours just to get out of Paris, I lost count of how many times I drove around the Arch de Triomphe trying to find the route north to the A1/E15. How I got the car home without a scratch was amazing.

In addition to the purchase of a new car we also bought new furniture, a huge corner unit and a large heavy coffee table with a tiled top, plus a bookcase full of Encyclopaedias, god knows why, we certainly fell for that one. Understandably all this was on HP or some kind of finance. By the summer of 1980 we were more than ready to go home on our annual summer leave. We hadn't slept for six months, well it most certainly felt like it. Linda was looking forward to introducing the newest member of our family to both our proud parents. Although the journey home was well worth it, it was quite an ordeal. This was the first time we had travelled any great distance with a young baby. As all new parents will know, there is no handbook, *"well none we had on our bookshelf"*, you just have to learn as you go. My mum had always told me that when I was a kid, I was a bit of a skriker (*Oldham slang meaning constantly crying*), well it was now payback.

The Best Loser

Most kids tend to sleep quite well when traveling in the back of a car... not a chance. The first leg of the journey was from Minden to Zeebrugge, he cried all the way there. We had a short respite on the ferry, until someone else's kid started. As you can imagine annual leave meant that almost everyone was going on leave, especially all those wanting to show off their new babies. It was like a crèche on the upper deck of the Zeebrugge to Dover ferry. The experienced squaddie travellers never rushed home on the first day of annual leave, they knew that the ferries would be full of that years brood of new-borns, all testing there little lungs.

When we returned from summer leave we started our training for an operational tour in Northern Ireland, my first of many. This meant weeks away training on the various ranges at Sennelager and yet more separation from my young family.

We deployed to Belfast in early November. It was going to be our first Christmas apart. Linda was not too keen on spending that Christmas alone and made the long journey back home to her mums on a coach, with a 10 month old baby strapped to her chest. And I thought the drive home with a crying baby on the back seat was hard. (*"Aren't mums brilliant"*).

Chapter 27

Belfast 80-81

Throughout my career I spent quite a few years on various operations in Northern Ireland. That first tour was both exciting and at times quite dangerous. Belfast in 1980/81 was the era of the Hunger Strikes, H-Block demonstrations, the dirty protest and infamous Mr Bobby Sands. The training we received at the famous Tin City Urban Warfare Ranges in Sennelager was without doubt the best preparation you could have. The mock village was very realistic, what made it more authentic was the guys and girls who volunteered for "Civpop". The mock riots gave you a taster of what to expect on the streets of Belfast, *"well almost"*. Most of the mock patrols we carried out were filmed on CCTV. On occasions we were identified by the numbers painted on the back of our Flak Jackets. The DS *(directing staff)*, took great pleasure in pointing out your mistakes, during the morning re-run of the previous day's events. It was a bit like TV Burp, or You've been framed but without Harry Hill, although at times just as entertaining in a serious kind of way.

By the time we arrived we were trained to the highest level. We had prepared for this deployment for almost a year. Nonetheless no amount of training can prepare you for that feeling you get when you first run out of the camp gates with your loaded rifle in your hand, as you hard target (zig, zag), for the first 50 to 100 metres. After a week or two patrolling through the streets of Belfast it all seemed so natural, to be honest it just becomes another job. If you spent time worrying about things you would be a nervous wreck.

During this first tour we spent the first three months operating out of Macroy Park. A small Company base which was situated on the Whiterock Road, close the junction of the famous Falls Road, quite notorious in its day. A time when there was always something going on, it's fair to say that in some areas we were not welcome. The history of the troubles in Northern Ireland in particular Belfast have been well documented over the years, by both soldiers, media types and journalists alike. Before sitting down to write this book I very rarely discussed what I experienced or did while I was there. I suppose it was always something that was drummed into us. Even when we were together with other members of the regiment we very rarely talked about things, if you did, someone would sarcastically say, *"pull up a sandbag"*, implying that this fucker is telling tales. Most of the time those people telling the tales were either exaggerating or not even there at all, Walter Mitty or Billy Liar types, the dreamers, we have all met them at some point in our lives.

Although Northern Ireland played a big part in my career I still find it hard to talk about. I suppose the truth was that at any time you could be shot at, blown up, seriously injured or killed, it wasn't something you talked about with your wife or members of your family. These were things that happened to other people you don't ever expect them to happen to you. I am not saying that you become complacent, quite the opposite, not only are you looking out for yourself you are also looking after your mates back. Even more so when you are a junior commander (*Brick Commander*), you are also responsible for the safety of the other three members of the patrol, they are actually following and taking their lead from you. The responsibility soon becomes very real indeed. We patrolled the streets in multiples of twelve, three four man teams working independently, while at the same time in a position to offer mutual support to the other teams om the ground. After a while it all becomes so natural (*routine*), although inside the adrenalin is pumping through your body.

Over the years I have lost count of how many times the media have commented on the death of soldiers, both in Northern Ireland, Iraq and more recently Afghanistan, quoting that he died whilst on a routine patrol, as if he was just crossing the road. The word routine implies that something is, dull, repetitive, mundane or predictable. Routine seems to trivialise their death, in my opinion all soldiers who are killed whilst on patrol in any conflict are quite simply killed in action.

Most of the patrols in the urban areas of Northern Ireland lasted anything from two to three hours and involved a number of key tasks. For example setting up a vehicle check point (VCP), tasked with stopping and searching cars. The primary aim of any patrol was to gather information, no matter how small or insignificant it may seem at the time. Undoubtedly those two or three hour patrols quite often turned into much longer periods out on the ground, especially when there was a major incident.

When we weren't patrolling we were sleeping or pumping iron in the small gym, which in most cases was just a small vacant room with a blue five station multi gym that just about fitted in the room. It was here where I got the taste for bodybuilding.

During the final three months we moved from our base in Macroy Park to a larger base closer to the City Centre of Belfast, Gridwood Park, on the Crumlin Road. From here we patrolled the Ardoyne, Unity Flats, New Lodge and sections of the City Centre. We also manned a number of OP's (*observation posts*), and Sangers (*fortified towers*). I celebrated my 21st Birthday sat in a Sanger at the top of Falx Street Mill, it was just another day on the calendar. Some of these Sangers like the one at the mill were self-contained. A location where we would spend a few days at a time, these were also prone to attack as they represented key points of occupation in the eyes of the IRA.

Almost all units serving in Northern Ireland during the height of the troubles would expect a number of major incident, and like most, during this particular tour, we had our fair share. It's difficult to explain the feeling you get when you are just a few streets away from a major explosion as you walk through the city centre of Belfast. When the bomb goes off there are a number of things that immediately cross your mind, the truth is, there is one little voice inside your head that says, "*shit we are going to be out here all night now sat on a fuckin cordon*". Fortunately my first experience of being in the close proximity to a large explosion resulted in no one being killed.

Sadly during this tour on the 25th January 1981 we lost a member of the battalion, Phillip Barker. He was shot in the head at point blank range and killed, while manning one of the checkpoints in the city centre. Phillip was from Oldham and the guy I met on the train when I first joined the battalion. When the incident involves someone you know very well it makes everything so real, it was one of those incidents that could have happened to anyone of us. Perhaps this was also one of the images within my subconscious that prevented me from doing something stupid, while at the low points in my life and during my most vulnerable moments. On the whole, the tour was a good start to my career, giving me an opportunity to prove my worth as a junior commander.

At the end of the tour we returned to Germany, Linda and young Mark re-joined me, and once again we enjoyed family life in Germany, albeit briefly. As we soon embarked on a number of major exercises on Soltau Plain, the home of mechanized training in Germany. By the end of the summer of 1982 we deployed to BATUS in Canada for four weeks. This was a major training exercise and was the culmination of a mechanized units training.

Prior to the move to BATUS I was promoted to Corporal and was now a section commander. No longer the driver of the 432, I now had the second best seat in the APC and commanded the vehicle from the cupola (*a kind of turret*) just behind the driver. The training we conducted was a large scale live firing Battlegroup exercise, supported by Battle Tanks, Recce and Combat Engineers.

At the end of each day we would form up in what was known as a leaguer position, the vast open spaces of this part of Canada where perfect for this formation, it also gave you a true account of the size of a full Battlegroup. Basically we lined up in straight lines in unit formation. A chance to relax in the sun, clean our kit and prepare for the next phase of the battle. It was during one of these leaguers where I was almost shot by a driver, who was sat in the back of the APC cleaning his rifle. (*This is a pull up a sandbag moment, although quite true*).

I was sitting on the ground at the back of the vehicle, talking to a few friends, and catching some rays, topping up my tan. The heavy rear door was open at an angle, the driver was sat inside on the opposite side facing the open door. All soldiers are taught the NSPs (Normal Safety percussions) something you carry out before you attempt to clean or strip the weapon down. One of the first things you do is to remove the Magazine, cock the weapon to remove the live round that may be in the chamber, you then check that the chamber is clear. Once it's clear you then squeeze the trigger, this releases the spring, so you can now strip the weapon down. Basically he failed to remove the magazine, from his rifle, he simply cocked the weapon and squeezed the trigger, BANG!! The round ricocheted off the back door and whistled just millimetres past my head. There was one immediate thought that entered my head, I had just survived my first tour in Northern Ireland and this Fucker was trying to kill me while I was enjoying the sun in Canada. Twat... was the second thought followed by immediate removal of the weapon from his hands, followed by a couple of well justified punches to his head.

Chapter 28

Time in the Sun

The words "End Ex" rang out over the vast plans of the dusty training area, as the message over the radio was repeated down the chain of command like a popular re-tweet from a well-known celebrity... For us the battle was over and it was time to take some well-earned R&R. This was a four day break from the grind of mechanized warfare. On this occasion we were left to our own devices, some lads hired cars and travelled south across the border to Montana in the USA, mainly to boast that they had visited America, chalking up another country on the bragging rights map. I on the other hand along with three of my mates travelled northwest to Calgary, a four hour coach trip on a Greyhound Bus. An experience in itself, as we travelled at speed down the open road of the Trans-Canada Highway.

Why Calgary? Well it was the time of the annual Calgary Stampede, this was the height of the Rodeo season, a chance to fulfil a childhood dream. As I looked out from my window across this wilderness of open spaces, with the picturesque mountains in the distance. I caught a glimpse of my reflection in the window. As I smiled to myself, those memories of running around the playground chanting *"all join on for Cowboys and Indians"* came flooding back. I was finally going to get a real glimpse into the life of a modern cowboy.

The excitement of jumping on a bus with just a clean shirt a few pairs of socks and pants, washing and shaving kit, all stuffed, OK *neatly folded*, into a small bag was a great feeling of freedom. We often forget how lucky we were to be able to do things like this, as I was often reminded by my wife. This was not a package holiday planned in advance, this was just a group of mates jumping on a bus taking pot luck. On arrival in Calgary our first task was to find somewhere to stay, we had no idea how big the place was. It was a metropolis of tall shiny buildings; everything seemed to be so clean and fresh. We eventually found the type of accommodation we could afford and checked into our rooms. Our next mission was to find some food, like the USA the Canadians love their food, and everything on the menu is supersized. Understandably we were all familiar with McDonalds' but we found something new, a Mr Sub, the original chain of the famous Canadian Submarine sandwich, now copied by the Subway chain, *(but very much smaller)* the sandwich that is. The original submarine sandwich was huge. I remember waking up the next day and I still had two thirds left from the one I bought the night before. We lived on those things for 3 days. The rodeo/stampede was a great day out, it was on for over a week and was everything I expected, Cowboys, Indians and rodeo clowns.

As with all these trips away or holidays as my wife called them, you couldn't go back home empty handed. So with what money I had left I bought a pair of handmade authentic Indian Moccasins, made by real Indians, well that's what they told me in the shop as I handed over my $35.

These were not for me I'm not that selfish, these were tiny baby moccasins perfect for my little boy. What I failed to take into account was that they would have fitted him perfectly before I left, but as we know kids grow fast and by the time we returned they simply made great ornaments and were placed on the bookcase.

Writing this book has reminded me that I have been fortunate to take R&R or take part in Adventuress Training Exercises in some beautiful places, all at the cost to the MOD. My most memorable being visits to Kenya and Jamaica. The trip to Kenya was amazing, we were serving there as part of a training exercise *"Grand Prix"*. This was primarily another live firing exercise, with a bit of jungle training thrown in for good measure. We also had an opportunity to see much more of the amazing landscape and take in everything Kenya has to offer as a holiday destination. We arrived in Kenya in late December 1989, landing at Nairobi on the 27th of December. On arrival we travelled north to Nayuki, crossing the Equator, where we all naturally jumped out and posed for photographs like excited tourists, pointing to the sign that read *"Equator Nanyuki 6389 feet"*, crossing the Equator isn't something you do every day. Our final destination was the British Army base in Nanyuki just a few miles northwest of Mount Kenya. I was part of the advance party so we arrived a couple of weeks before the remainder of the Battalion. At the time I was a CQMS (*Company Quartermaster Sergeant*). It was my job along with my three storemen to look after all the administrative needs of the company, basically I was the guy who got stuff. I am not sure if my army colleagues would agree with me but this was in my opinion one of the best appointments I had, although at times it was quite demanding. During the first phase of the exercise it was our job to set up a tented camp close to a small Masia settlement, at a place called Dol Dol in the Rift Valley. This was a small remote African village with a mixture of traditional huts on the outskirts of the village, plus a number of corrugated whitewashed breeze block buildings which formed the hub of the village.

Prior to leavening for Kenya I had just spent Christmas with Linda, young Mark, and our latest arrival six month old, baby Tom. At the time we were living in a married quarter in the beautiful city of Canterbury. This was one of the rare occasions when we were all together, although Linda wasn't too pleased to see me leave for Brize Norton the day after Boxing Day. Especially when the majority of our friends and neighbours stayed home and enjoyed the remainder of the Christmas and New Year break with their families.

Arriving in Dol Dol was a real eye opener, which was over a two and half hours' drive from Nanyuki, along what was at times was just a dirt track. I felt like one on those celebrities arriving for the first time in a poverty stricken township during an appeal for comic relief. I remember seeing a kid playing with a coat hanger that had been expertly crafted and shaped into what can only be described as small truck, he was happily dragging it around on a piece of string. This was in stark contrast to watching Mark just a few days earlier opening his presents on Christmas day. I remember spending a small fortune that year on the latest

Transformers, and here I was in a Kenya just a few days later watching a kid play just as excitedly with a coat hanger, which was without doubt the best transformer I had seen, (*priceless*). I can clearly see why celebrities get completely overwhelmed by what they see when they visit places like this, we forget how lucky we are, it's also a crying shame that we also quickly forget as this feeling soon subsides, as we get on with our own lives. Something I may have mentioned in an earlier chapter.

Each day I would travel along that dusty dirt track in my open top Land Rover from Dol Dol, back to Nanyuki, for fresh water and supplies. All in all over a five hour return trip. On the first day I would pass villagers, young and old all walking that very same route, some taking days to get to their destination. Kids would also run after the Land Rover as we raced down the track like rally drivers on the final stages of a race. As I looked through the mirrors I could see that they were still running, not stopping or giving up until we threw some rations, biscuits or chocolate, from the window. I am sure we helped to train a few Olympic champions along the way, these kids were fast. One day I made the fatal mistake of stopping to give an old guy a lift, he looked about 90 years old. I took him all the way to Nanyuki. I just hoped that's where he wanted to go and wasn't just waiting to cross the track, as the conversation never got past "Jambo my friend". A few days later he was waiting for me as I passed the same spot, being the kind hearted soul I am, we stopped and from nowhere his wife appeared from the undergrowth with a goat. I thought you cheeky fuckers, but let them both get on, by the end of the week we had a truck full of pensioners, it was like a geriatric safari.

After our time at Dol Dol we returned to Nanyuki, our company then had the opportunity to carry out a spot of Platoon adventure training. Some went off on a three day camel safari, while others tackled Mount Kenya. I was fortunately left to my own devices as I was not officially part of a platoon. I decide to go on my own Safari, after seeing a map/leaflet for the popular destination of Samburu Lodge. It was only a short two hour drive northeast from where we were. Just before leaving the RSM asked me where I was going, this was one of those occasions when you wished you had lied, *"sounds good I think I will come with you"*. Then the CSM who was supposed to be joining a Platoon tackling Mount Kenya said *"sounds good to me I'll come with you, I've got a chest infection so I can't take the altitude on the mountain"*. A thought entered my head, here we go again another geriatric safari with these two fuckers in the back. The truth was, it was just brilliant, we had the freedom to simply go where we wanted, once we arrived at the Samburu National Reserve. With no official guide, we went in search of elephants and rhinos. It was quite an eventful trip and, with my camera around my neck I was ready to snap some wildlife shots, worthy of the great Mr Attenborough himself. Within the first few minutes of entering the reserve we saw a cheetah about a 50 metres from the Land Rover, we jumped out to take photographs, then realised what we had just done and immediately scrambled back in, forgetting that these fuckers can run up to 75 mph. We eventually got to see the wild elephants crossing the river, we were also ambushed by large troop of baboons as we crossed the bridge close the lodge itself. Once you are at the lodge you also get close to the crocks especially during feeding time. I felt slightly guilty as we sat at the bar drinking a cold Tusker, surrounded by honeymooners and holiday makers alike who had no doubt spent a small fortune just getting here. My thoughts then turned to my poor wife sat at home, so I put down my cold beer, looked across at my friends then raised my glass and said… *"To the wife, god bless ya luv"*. She won't read this…

In addition to this little trip to Samburu Lodge we also travelled to Lake Naivasha for more adventure training, canoeing with hippos and climbing volcanoes. While we were there a group of us also went to visit the Elsamere Conservation Centre, the home of the famous George and Joy Adamson of Born Free fame. We got a private guided tour which included tea and cakes on the lawn which overlooked the picturesque lake. Doesn't sound that exciting, it wasn't, but come on cake and tea on the lawn that's just heavenly. My lasting memory of this exercise/holiday (*"my wife's words"*), was during the R&R phase, we flew from Nairobi in a light aircraft a forty seater, which at one point I thought wasn't going to make it, before landing at Mombasa in the south. As I walked across the white sand looking out across the Indian ocean I made a promise to myself that I would go back to Kenya one day and experience all those things again with Linda.

The trip to Jamaica was just as good, by this time I was a Company Sergeant Major (CSM), in charge of the 140 men who accompanied me on this trip, along with a handful of

Senior NCOs', junior officers and a Company Commander, who was a great guy. Getting there was an experience in itself as we travelled from Heathrow on a civilian flight to Kingston courtesy of British Airways. If you thought travelling with kids was difficult try being responsible for 140 troops on a ten hour flight to Jamaica especially when drink is ready available, let alone free. I was up and down the aisles like a demented trolley dolly for the first few hours, making sure that they weren't abusing the hospitality of British Airways, before returning to my seat in business class to finish my glass of Champagne, (*hypocrite*).

This trip to Jamaica was part of an ongoing exchange with the Jamaican Defence Force, named exercise "Red Stripe", any exercise named after a popular beer can't be bad. We arrived in Jamaica without any problems and travelled to our base at Port Antonio, situated to the north of the island. Across the small bay was Navy Island, once the home of legendary actor Errol Flynn. While we were there in 1992, it was a popular holiday destination, sadly at the time of writing this book I learned that it fell into a state of disrepair, what a shame. While we were in the Caribbean we had the opportunity to carry out some excellent training including a short phase of Jungle warfare training which was conducted by three members of the SAS, one of which was a former training partner (*soldier B*), and fellow Fusilier who had passed selection back in 1988. During our tour in Cyprus we trained for SAS selection, but more on that later... One of the most memorable times in Jamaica was flying down the black river in a Huey Helicopter with a crazy pilot from the Jamaican Defence Force, it was like a scene from Apocalypse Now. He told us that the chopper we were flying in was actually in service during the Vietnam War, he wasn't kidding as it was held together with black masking tape, (*I'm not joking either*). I had been in many helicopters over the years and nothing really phased me, but this guy was a nutcase, his party piece was to dip the nose of the aircraft and then the tail rotor in a rocking motion so it was inches off the sea, in fact at one point the blades of the rotor skimmed the water, as we came into land on the beach, (*crazy mother fucker*).

Once again we also had the opportunity to take a spot of R&R when the training phase of the exercise was over. The majority of the troops travelled to Ocho Rios near Montego Bay, while me and a group of SNCOs, took the short taxi ride to Dragon Bay, where they filmed the Tom Cruise film Cocktail. "*If my wife is reading this, as I said love it was pretty shit*". There was nothing to do but play volley ball on the beach and drink cocktails, as we laid in the baking sun, listening to Reggae music at full volume. One tune in particular comes to mind, by Chaka Dems and Pliers, "Murder She Wrote". So on that note I think I had better end this chapter here as I think she'll kill me when she reads this.

Chapter 29

Not Ireland Again

Unfortunately my time in the army wasn't all volley ball, cocktails and sandy beaches. Just before the end of our four year posting to Germany back in October 1983, I was posted back to Northern Ireland. This time I was a young twenty three year old sergeant working independently as part of the Intelligence Platoon, deployed to Aughnacloy, a small market town close to the border a couple of miles north of Monaghan. I arrived four months before the battalion, my primary role was to provide continuity and intelligence support to the rifle companies who patrolled the areas of East Tyrone. While at the same time acting as liaison between the Army and the RUC (*Royal Ulster Constabulary*). It wasn't a role that suited being accompanied by your family due to the nature of the job, as it required full commitment plus almost 24/7 support to troops on the ground, so Linda moved back to the UK.

I spent the first six weeks working alongside my predecessor, a thirty five year old long haired Staff Sergeant from the Cheshire Regiment. It's fair to say that he was looking forward to the end of his tour. This guy had done a great job and was a tough act to follow. We spent most of the time driving around the countryside of east Tyrone, in an unmarked car, as he pointed out all the hotspots of previous incidents. All in all, it was an area of over 300 square miles. During this time of the handover he also introduced me to various key members of the RUC/Special

Branch, while attending various intelligence meetings and briefings. As we travelled from Cookstown and Dungannon in the north, to Clougher, Ballygawley, Aughnacloy and Caleden in the south.

I soon realised that there was quite a lot to learn before my own unit arrived, not to mention getting accustomed to the drinking culture. It's surprising how much you can learn by standing at the bar after a meeting. It didn't take me long to work out that although we were all on the same side, it was quite evident that some intelligence services were keeping some of their cards close to their chest. By the time my own unit arrived at the Battalions main base in Ballykelly, I was supporting a beard and had grown my hair. I was now in permanent residence at the small base in Aughnacloy. This is where I had a large private room with all the home comforts, including a large aquarium of various tropical fish, left to me by my predecessor, plus some basic instructions on how to look after them. Within a few months they were all dead, I always seemed to lose a few when cleaning the tank, perhaps something to do with the water temperature. As I may have poached a few, while others made their escape down the plug hole to freedom in the south. I suppose fish weren't my thing. So I replaced them with a couple of terrapins, called Bodie & Doyle, (*names changed to protect their identity*), which I purchased from a pet shop in Dungannon, these were much more exciting, and easy to clean.

The view out of my window wasn't much to look at, as it was quite simply a 12ft breeze block blast wall just inches from the window. On the other side of the wall was the parameter fence, beyond that a chicken farm, which omitted an almost unbearable stink, especially during the summer months. Fortunately I spent very little time in my room. Most days involved driving to and from meetings with various members of the intelligence services, this was something I often did alone, as I felt less conspicuous. I suppose I felt more in control and if something did happen I only had to think about my own safety.

To be honest it's a difficult job description to explain, for a number of reasons, what I can say is that the bulk of my workload involved quite a lot of report writing.

The separation from my young family was hard at times, especially as I missed those important earlier years of Mark growing up. Not to mention three consecutive Christmases, Birthdays and Anniversaries. Looking back now I can see that I was totally selfish, by putting the job before my family; however as this type of appointment doesn't come around that often, it was in my opinion a real career move. I continually told myself that I was doing this for my family, the reality being I was perhaps doing it for me. The job gave me an opportunity to shine as an individual, as I was the only one doing that particular job. Every month a new company of 120 troops would arrive at the base. It was my job to brief them and keep them up to date on all matters of intelligence, setting tasks for patrol commanders, and collating the information they brought back. I would also on occasion accompany them on the ground, especially on covert patrols. Each company was also supported by a small team of collators and an office manager, all fellow members of the Intelligence Platoon. The office managers were all SNCOs, experienced Staff Sergeants, all with many more years' service under their belts than me. One guy in particular became my good friend and a kind of mentor, on occasion offering me sound advice, in a way a big brother type of figure. He was a larger than life character, a guitar playing Geordie named Cloughie, the type of guy who was the life and soul of any party.

One of the main landmarks close to the base was a PVCP, (*Permanent vehicle Checkpoint*), this was on the border between Aughnacloy and Monaghan in the south. Over the years it had been attacked many times, plus there were countless serious incidents in this area, especially along the stretch of the border we were responsible for. Therefore border patrols were part of the main focus for troops deployed in this area. Another primary concern were the off duty members of the RUC, and soldiers from the UDR (*Ulster Defence Regiment*), who lived in the areas close to the border. I got to know many of them personally, as I worked alongside them and socialised with them quite often. They also shared the camp in Aughnacloy and conducted their own patrols. I learned so much from them, especially during the earlier months. They were all members of A Company 8 UDR, mostly part time soldiers, who operated on a similar basis to the TA (*Territorial Army*) in the UK. The A Company Bar was a frequent respite from the daily routine, and we all know that the Irish like a good old sing song. So along with my new best pal Cloughie, we would entertain our audience as a duo, a poor man's Robson & Jerome. To be honest Cloughie did most of the singing I looked after the drinks. Although you can't go mad on a two pint limit, as this was the norm for soldiers on active duty.

It wasn't long before I experienced the first serious incident of this tour. This was a shooting of an off duty part timer from A Company. He was ambushed as he drove up the track to his farm house, just a couple of miles from the base. His wife and child where in the car at the time. I arrived at the scene about 30 minutes after the incident along with some members of the RUC. I had experienced similar scenes during my previous tour in Belfast but nothing really prepares for what you see so soon after an incident has occurred. He had been shot in the head, as he was about to park his car at the top track close to his house. His wife was sitting in the back with the baby, fortunately they escaped serious injury as she managed to escape through the rear window of the car which disintegrated as the bullets passed through it. I don't think I need to go into graphic detail, as I am sure we have all seen films that illustrate the impact of someone being shot in the head. Miraculously though he survived his injuries and within less than twelve months he was back in the bar having a drink with his friends. He never returned to active duty as his injuries left him with slight damage to his brain, which effected his speech and left him with limited movement down one side of his body. Sadly he wasn't so lucky, as I later discovered that a few years later a second attempt on his life proved fatal.

It soon became apparent that life in Aughnacloy was going to be busy, as there were many more incidents within our TAOR (*Tactical Area of Responsibility*). Time off was a rarity for me and getting home was difficult, if I did it was only for a few days at a time, such was the nature of the job. Mark was growing up fast but I wasn't there to see it. I was well and truly married to the job, constantly telling myself that all this was for the better. Life in Aughnacloy had become so important to me. I thrived on the individuality, at the end of each rotation I would be called upon to return to the main base in Ballykelly to conduct a major briefing to an audience of officers and troops. I was starting to enjoy the attention, as I stood on stage of the large auditorium, while I dissected previous incidents, to build the intelligence picture for their forthcoming deployment, a bit like a senior detective on crime drama. By the end of the first year I was in full flow, more confident than ever.

It was at this time when I was first asked to perform for money, not sexually, I kept my clothes on, this was comedy. (*Note to the Taxman, I did it for free and no money exchanged hands*). On this occasion I was asked once again to act as MC/Compare for the entertainment after a games night between the Corporals and Sergeants Mess. Let me explain… A "Games Night" is something the messes would lay on occasionally, basically these where based on the traditional pub games of darts, dominoes, pool, Kerplunk! To be honest it was an excuse to get pissed, without the wives tagging along, as they were told, "*Its compulsory love, I've been ordered to go, honest*". Each mess would take it in turn to host the other, and quite often the culmination of the night would also include some form of entertainment. On this occasion it was the Corporals turn to play host, and the event was to be held in the large NAFFI at the base in Ballykelly. The entertainment for the night was to be two exotic dancers, (*strippers*), plus yours truly. It was my job to introduce them and fill in with a few blue gags during the breaks. The real gag was that, there were actually no strippers, but no one told the Warrant Offers & Sergeants Mess members, who had turned out in force. To be honest there were only three of us in the know, the PMC, (*President of the mess committee*) and the PEC, (*President of the entertainments committee*) from the corporals' mess. The NAAFI was crammed to the rafters with over 200 blokes on heat, there was only one woman in the place and she was serving drinks behind the bar.

When the games night ended I took my place on stage with only one thought in my head *"these fuckers and going to kill me"*. I started my set with my bow tie hanging from my collar and all the buttons of my shirt undone to the waist. I pushed my way through the curtains on the stage, and wiping my brow and removing the lipstick from my cheek, I went into my routine...

"You are going to love these two, they are f**king crazy, especially the blonde one". Re-buttoning my shirt I re-enacted the scene, by telling a well-known gag. It was visual comedy so you will have to use your imagination.

Blonde Stripper: ooooooh Mark have you seen the PEC from the corporals mess? ...As she ran her fingers through my hair.

Me: No love! …in my best Northern accent.

Blonde Stripper: ooooooh Mark have you seen the PMC from the corporals Mess? …As she now ran her fingers through my beard and squeezed my face.

Me: No love!

Blonde Stripper: oooooh Mark have you seen the PEC from the Sergeants Mess? …As she had now started to unbutton my shirt, rubbing her hands through the hair on my chest.

Me: No love honest!

Blonde Stripper: oooooh Mark have you seen the PMC from the Sergeants Mess? As she continued to rub her hands through the hairs on my chest, tweaking my nipples.

Me: No pet honest man! …in my best Geordie accent.

Blonde Stripper: ooooh Mark have you seen the RSM? …As she now pushed both hands down my pants and started rubbing the hair in my lower regions.

Me: No love honest! …my eyes rolling to the back of my head.

Blonde Stripper: Well when you do… tell him there is no F**king Toilet Paper in the SHITHOUSE! … Trust me it was much better than it appears in this book.

The place erupted with laughter, fortunately it was the first time they had heard that joke. Without pausing for the applause I unzipped my trousers and said… *"I was so excited I had to get my cock out"*, only to reveal the head of a rubber chicken which I had stuffed down the front of my trousers earlier. As I pulled on it stretching the rubber neck, I looked around at the audience and noticed the girl at the bar, the whole place was in fits of laughter, as I turned to her direction and said, *"its OK love it's a pullet"* as I whipped out the rubber chicken. I then immediately went into my now famous chicken joke routine.

I had won them over they were mine, it was a great feeling, I felt like a true professional. After finishing my first set I was ready to introduce the real reason they had all turned out in force. *"Gentlemen and the Lesbian at the bar, only joking love, for your pleasure, and for one night only please welcome on stage the unforgettable Blonde Bombshell Patricia!.* The place erupted again as the music to Patricia the stripper by Chris de Burge stated to play. Then out strolled one of the biggest corporals in the mess, dressed in a long blonde wig, stockings and suspenders, fishnet tights and high heel shoes, he wasn't the best drag queen, more pantomime dame than anything. As I now watched from the side of the stage, I thought this is it, this is where I get lynched. The faces in the audience told their own story, first there was the disappointment/anger that they had been setup and then from many who were married men, the image of relief. As they now didn't have to face their wives', who by this stage would have known that they had gone to the games night to see strippers and not some fat bloke in a dress. If there was a hint of a female woman in the flesh, they would have found out quicker than a viral video on Facebook, even though it hadn't yet been invented. Finally a voice shouted out *"Fuck me… its BRASSA!"*, then in unison a group started chanting those immortal words, *"Get your tits out, get your tits out, get your tits out for the lads… get your tits out for the lads?"*. The night was a resounding success, and launched me into my new found career as the camp comedian, not in a gay way of course.

I returned to Ballykelly on a number of occasions for various functions, mess dinners, to either host, compare or simply perform a few gags. It helped to pass the time and gave me a break from the reality of what was really going on in Northern Ireland at the time. I know many professional comedians have also said this, but when I was in front of an audience I became someone else, or was this the real me trying to get out. There was no doubt that this period in my life helped to forge my military career. Towards the end of my time in Aughnacloy I was approached by another military intelligence group, with a view to staying on, for the record I seriously considered it.

I had been in Ireland for almost three years, by the time I was ready for the handover. Separated from family, with only brief visits home, Linda had been great during this time and supported me all the way. If I had told her that I was staying on who knows what might have happened. Plus the Battalion was about to deploy to Cyprus for two years on completion of our time in Northern Ireland. I think I owed it to them both, as this would mean we would be back together, plus the weather and lifestyle in Cyprus is far better than that in Northern Ireland and Oldham. So I turned down the opportunity to stay on, and focused on the handover to a former member of the SAS, a nice guy called Ben.

The Best Loser

It was now my turn to pass on the knowledge and guide him through the first few months of his deployment. It wasn't long before he got a true taste of the unpredictable nature of the job. We had spent the day travelling around some of the key areas of the patch. At five o'clock on Saturday the 7th of December 1986 I took him to Ballygawley RUC Station, to introduce him to some of the guys I had worked with over the years, some of which were now close friends. We left about an hour later and returned to Aughnacloy for our evening meal.

At 6.45pm I was lying on my bed watching TV, when everything suddenly went black... followed immediately by an almighty explosion, all the power had gone off... then I heard the contact report over the radio, which one of the platoon sergeants had left switched on in the corridor. The report came from troops on the ground close to Ballygawley, they were a visiting unit carrying out a patrol on the A4 (*Omagh Road*), just north of Ballygawley. They reported that the explosion came from the direction of the RUC station. All the power was now off in the camp as it took a few minutes for the emergency generator to kick in. I rushed to the ops room to grab the Company Commander, we both jumped in my car and took the short four mile drive to the RUC station, we were amongst the first to arrive on the scene, closely followed by our medical team. The station had been completely destroyed. Two RUC officers where lying close to the gates, it was clear from their injures that they were unlikely to survive, as the medic tried unsuccessfully to revive them. The other officers in the station at the time also suffered injuries, but survived the blast, as they managed to get to the back of the building before the IED exploded.

Just less than 45 minutes ago I was having coffee with these guys, and now I was watching two of them die in the street. I had never felt so helpless. It wasn't until many years later that I finally broke down, while looking down at my brother lying in a hospital bed, having just returned from his operation to stop the bleeding on his brain. It was made clear that he would be lucky to survive. It was at this point that my thoughts returned to this moment in my life. They had both been shot in the head as the bombers left the station, after planting the bomb. (*This is something I have never really talked about before not even to my wife.*) As we learned quite quickly that at least four men quite calmly parked their car just opposite the RUC station. One got out of the car armed with an AK47, and positioned himself on a low flat roof just opposite to the gates. Two others took a beer keg from the back of the car walked to the gates and rang the bell. As the two offices approached the gates the guy on the roof opened fire. While the two men with the beer keg walked into the entrance of the building to plant the IED (*improvised explosive device*). They then returned to the car, but not before shooting the two offices in the head as they lay on the ground. It was without doubt a well-planned and well executed operation. Ballygawley RUC Station had been completely flattened by 200lb IED, contained in a single beer keg, placed just inside the entrance of the main building. As I stood there for a while looking at the destruction. My head was again firing on all cylinders, all the events from the many months prior to this attack now started to fall into place, all the snippets of information pieced together. It was like finally finding the lid to a jigsaw puzzle, prior to this event I had all the pieces but no clear picture to work on. This made the final three months of the tour the most interesting, although it was yet another Christmas separated from my family, something Linda had come to expect. The workload preparing for the handover kept me very busy. At the end of the tour I was awarded the GOC's commendation, (*General Officer Commanding Northern Ireland*), for the work I carried out while I was there, some people thought I deserved more. Nevertheless that award came much later, as there were many more tours of Northern Ireland to come.

Chapter 30

Back to Basics

When I finally left Aughnacloy I was 26 years old, although still quite young compared to many of fellow SNCOs, (*Senior Non Commissioned Officers*), however I had missed out on some of the key career courses associated with infantry soldiering, especially at platoon sergeant level. It was now time to shave off my beard get my hair cut and climb back on the promotion ladder. I was thrown back into the world of soldiering with a massive wakeup call. As I soon found myself standing on the drill square at Perbright, the home of the guards division. Six weeks on a Drill Instructors Course, was the best wakeup call you could have. Especially after spending almost three years in civvies, with long hair and a beard. It was like being back in basic training, but ten times worse. After the initial shock of being bounced around the drill square every morning, by some crazy drill instructor from the Coldstream Guards, I started to see the significance of it all. In a crazy way I started to enjoy it. To teach drill effectively you need a good sense of humour and a slightly crazy kind of personality. All the instructors were themselves larger than life characters, big loud shouty Fuckers, all looking for perfection in anything you did.

Attending this course taught me so much more than the aim of drill, which for the record is: (*To produce a soldier who is proud, alert, obedient, and also provides the basis of teamwork*). After all these years it is something which is still committed to memory. Once you got past the daily routine which always started with a room and kit inspection. Where we would all stand outside our own individual rooms, dressed in our best kit, praying that nothing would be picked up. Attention to detail was paramount, if the slightest thing was wrong, out of place, you would find yourself on show parade, which were a little different than those parades associated with basic training, as they were tame in comparison. This show parade required you and the offending item to be out on the square after breakfast attending yet another inspection. You would see some poor sod carrying his bed or his personal locker and all its contents, sometimes the contents of his whole room, out to the drill square for re-inspection. I saw one lad with a picture of his wife and asked why he was taking that out? He said that one of the tall shouty Fuckers had said that she was smiling, and no one smiles in here, so he was ordered to parade with his picture showing smile removed. So he had drawn a frown with a marker pen on the glass of the frame to show "SMILE REMOVED". It was all part of the game, and although carrying your bed outside isn't much fun especially when you have to get it all back in before the start of the first lesson, you very rarely make the same mistake twice. Some will argue, what's the point of all this? Isn't this just army bullshit? However attention to detail is without question the single most important factor in anything we do. It could also be said that this course tests your sense of character/humour. Six weeks of this routine and it all becomes second nature. I am sure that anyone reading this especially some of my fellow colleges' who have attended this course will agree when I say. That this was not only the most memorable course, and not just for drinking, and the huge mess bill, but one that helped to shape the person I later became, perhaps not always for the better.

The way in which drill is taught provides a sound foundation for any form of instruction. Everything is broken down into simple steps, each one mastered before you move on to the next. Some may argue that teaching someone to quite simply put one foot in front of the other may be considered a simple undertaking, but throw in a few left and right turns, give them a rifle to carry. Then throw in a few more drill movements that involve rifle drill and the whole thing can fall apart if the instruction isn't delivered in such a way that everyone understands the part they play.

After the drill course I returned home for a few days to help Linda pack up the house for our move to Cyprus, finally back together and on our way to a sunshine posting. We were told that the working day would start at seven and finish by lunchtime. Life in Cyprus was going to be so cushy, compared to the busy lifestyle I left behind in Northern Ireland. What a great way to get back together as a family after all the separation we endured during previous years of our marriage. Young Mark was also looking forward to getting away from the school he hated, he was now six years old, and I had missed so much of these important years in his little life. We arrived in Cyprus on a warm sunny day in mid-April, the house we moved into was fantastic, and without doubt our favourite married quarter. A large three bedroomed semidetached house at number 16

Durham Road, close to the camp at the sovereign base in Episkopi. As married quarters go this was at the top end of the scale, with large gardens both at the front and the rear, with orange and lime trees standing proud in the sunshine, it was perfect. The only problem was the tension in the Middle East was once again on the rise. Reagan & Gaddafi were not the best of pals, especially after bombs were dropped on Tripoli which in turn raised the alert state in Cyprus to an all-time high. Before we knew it we were erecting wire fences and building Sangers on the beaches close to RAF Akrotiri air base, and throughout other key points within the sovereign base. Our so called cushy posting was turned upside down. Within days of arriving I was deployed with my platoon to guard the radar installation at Mount Olympus high in the Troodos Mountains. We hadn't even had time to unpack our boxes, Linda was once again on her own, and life in Cyprus for the resident battalion was changed for ever. Those first few weeks were tough for her as she had to once again get used to the routine of me being away.

By the summer the alert state was lowered, so it wasn't long before we settled into the new routine. When we weren't deployed to guard the key points, life on the island was pretty good. The weather helped, plus the beach was less than three miles away. Mark quickly settled in school which was just at the end of the road, he was never so happy, and life in the army was good again. Well at least for a while. Until one quiet sunny Sunday afternoon in August, while sitting in our favourite restaurant enjoying our meal. It was a restaurant many of us used at the time, as it was actually cheaper to eat out. On this occasion our meal was interrupted by the arrival of two military Land Rover's which screamed to a halt in the dusty carpark. We were all told to return to camp, as there had been a terrorist attack by Lebanese extremists, who had just carried out a mortar and RPG7 attack *(rocket propelled grenade)*, on the Airbase at RAF Akrotiri, just a couple of miles away. The alert state was once again at its highest and we were soon back on active duty. Less than an hour later I was issuing live ammunition to my platoon as we waited to board helicopters before being deployed to support the Parachute Regiment north of the island, once again leaving our wives and families at home. It's fair to say that the first year was not what we had expected.

The second year in Cyprus was better, as I was selected to help to train young potential JNCO's *(junior non-commissioned officers)*. These were guys taking their first steps on the promotion ladder, just as I did back in 1979. It was an opportunity to influence these young minds, teaching the next generation of leaders/junior commanders. This would also mean working to a much more predictable timetable. However before doing this I had to return to the UK, to attend an instructors' course in Nuclear Biological and Chemical Warfare, at the infamous secret centre at Porton Down in Wiltshire. This meant another two weeks separated from my family. By this time Linda had got used to me being away again, the important thing Mark was happy at school, and seemed to be a much more confident little seven year old kid. Linda also had a great network of friends, so that two weeks away passed quite quickly, for us both.

When I returned I settled into my new job as a member of the Training Wing. It was at this time in my life when I was at my highest peak of fitness. I ran everywhere with a 50lb pack on my back, many of my friends thought I was training for SAS selection, the truth being, secretly I was. Cyprus offered the perfect training ground, especially the hills in the Troodos Mountains. I trained regularly with three of my friends, all of us with a burning desire to take the ultimate test. Passing selection for the Regiment was a desire I had had since the age of 22. When as a young impressionable corporal, I attended a Battlefield Survival course in Germany, a course run entirely by members of the SAS. At the time almost all young servicemen of the early eighties generation dreamt of joining the SAS, especially after seeing the raid on the Iranian Embassy in April 1980. This was the first time the general public got their first glimpse of the SAS in action, as the black figures abseiled down the front of the Iranian Embassy. They ended the six day siege in less than 12 minutes, it was all over for the terrorists. More importantly the world got to see how effective the elite British Special Forces were.

As serving soldiers the Battlefield and Combat Survival courses were the first real introduction to life as a member of the SAS, these courses were a form of internal recruiting. Almost all the other guys I attended the course with were planning on attending selection, at some point in the very near future, although this was not something you would shout from the rooftops, most were SNCOs and Officers. At 22 I was the youngest on the course and gained some valuable experience. Part of the course involved an element of escape and evasion. As we were split into four man patrol teams and spent five days without food, in the Bavarian hills evading capture from a Company of troops from the Canadian intelligence Corps. My fellow patrol teammates were a mixed bag of individuals, one a sergeant from the Green Jackets, he didn't say much, as he adopted the same approach as me, quiet unassuming, keeping ourselves to ourselves. The other a Lieutenant from the Engineers, he was a big rugby playing Irishman with a personality to match. Finally our patrol commander, a Captain from the Royal Ordnance Corps, there is only one way to describe him, he was a bit of knob, his name was Wiseman, unfortunately he didn't live up to his name. He made the mistake of telling the instructors he was attending selection in a few weeks' time, understandably this brought him some unnecessary attention. Prior to the escape and evasion phase of the course we carried out a number of tasks, these involved survival skills, everything from skinning rabbits, foraging for food to drinking your own pee, *mmm salty*. The instructors were all experienced members of B Squadron, from 22 SAS. One of the sergeants was involved in the operation at the Iranian Embassy, who I met some years later at an intelligence briefing in Northern Ireland. One of the other sergeants a huge man called Vince, who was later a member of the famous Bravo Two Zero incident in Iraq in 1991, along with *Andy McNabb. Sadly Vince didn't make it back and died of hypothermia in the desert during the withdrawal from their compromised position.

*Andy (Steven), was in training with us at Shorncliffe, IJLB in 1976. Shhhhhhhhhhhh don't tell anybody.

So ever since attending this course I often thought about trying for selection. I watched as many people I knew very well, who I thought quite capable, try but fail for one reason or another. Selection for the SAS is not easy, it starts with a three week endurance phase in the Brecon Beacons. Ending with a 40 mile trek over the highest peaks in the region, with a 55lb Bergen on your back, which you must complete in under 24hrs. If you make it through that phase it's off to the jungle in Brunei, for six weeks. Where you work in four man patrol teams, this is the most difficult phase and requires great mental strength and personal discipline. Many people fail during this phase. Finally selection is completed after a phase of Combat Survival, and tactical questioning, which is a nice way of saying interrogation.

If I learnt anything from my training on the Battlefield Survival course, it was that, to even consider trying for selection, preparation was key if you were to be in with the slightest chance of succeeding. I remember being told by one of the instructors that two years was the norm. He said, that's two years of continuous training, preparing yourself both physically and mentally, is what's required my young Jedi. So during my second year in Cyprus I felt almost ready to give it a good shot. My good friend who I will call Frank, because that was his name, and a fellow Training Wing instructor had tried for selection a few months earlier and had made to the jungle phase, but was RTUd (Returned to Unit), due to suffering a knee injury. He was trying again, and encouraged me to join him. The other two lads we trained with, who I will call soldier A and soldier B, Alan and Brian, ironically their real names, were also keen to give it a shot. All three eventually passed selection and became members of the elite Regiment 22 SAS. I on the other hand never even gave it a shot. I met them all again at various points in my career, they all asked why I never took up the challenge. I simply shrugged my shoulders and said I don't know. I met Brian again in Jamaica when I was a Company Sergeant Major, he was one of the SAS instructors assisting with the Jungle Training. I suppose my excuse now, was that I wanted to focus on my career with the Battalion, and not have to start all over again as a Trooper in the SAS.

The real truth of the matter was… I feared failure, I had never actually really failed anything up until that point in my life, but I feared failing selection. So I never actually submitted the application, physically I was more than ready. I suppose the main reason for not going at the time was that I actually didn't want to go through more separation. Family life in Cyprus during the second year was much better, as by this time we had settled into the routine. We had a nice house, I was driving a brand new car, young Mark was happy at school, Linda was too. I was also on the promotion ladder, yeah life was pretty good. So I didn't want to leave my family again and put them through yet more separation. Yeah OK, that's what I kept telling myself, the real truth being, I feared failure. After all I was the "Best Loser", so there was a good chance that despite all my efforts and preparation I would probably suffer an injury at a critical phase during the final exercise or something. Nevertheless this didn't stop me from telling myself that I was good enough, and if I wanted to I could make it in the SAS.

There is an old saying "better to have tried and failed, than not to try at all". Mine at the time was "better not try something you might fail and beat yourself up about it for the rest of your life". This best loser thing was starting to have an effect on me. I suppose constantly being told that first is first and second is fucking nowhere starts to resonate after a while.

All through my army career I regretted not giving it a shot, despite being successful in my own right, well as far as the military career goes, that is. Perhaps if back then I had read Susan Jeffers book, "Feel the Fear and Do it Anyway" this would be a different story.

Chapter 31

Promotion, Pneumonia and a Big Bang!

As we approached the end of the tour in Cyprus I was promoted to Staff Sergeant (Colour Sergeant), I was to become the CQMS (Company Quartermaster Sergeant) of Z Company. Understandably if you are not familiar with the Army ranking structure and what this appointment means it's difficult to understand the significance of this promotion, or know what a CQMS does? Basically the overall job description for this appointment is that, it's your job is to get stuff, something I mentioned earlier. I can't remember the full job description for an infantry CQMS, but I am sure somewhere it said that it was your job to provide the unobtainable. Like Morgan Freemans character in Shawshank Redemption "Red", you were the go to guy, basically if the company commander wanted it for the troops it was your job to get it. You also looked after and maintained all the G1098 equipment, this is all the equipment used on field operations. Reaching this rank at the age of twenty eight was a significant step on the promotion ladder, putting me on track to make it to Company Sergeant Major before the age of thirty two. Looking back, this job was ranked as one of the best appointments I had, although quite tasking and demanding at times, above all I loved the independence it offered.

We had arrived back in the UK in early-January 1988. Linda was two months pregnant with our Tom. We landed at Brize Norton and boarded coaches to take us to our new barracks in Canterbury, as we drove through the Kent countryside the aftermath of the storms of October 87 were still evident, as we passed numerous giant fallen trees, uprooted by the strong winds the weather men never predicted. We arrived at our new married quarter, a brand new three bedroomed house, on a private estate at the back of camp. We had a few days off to settle in before we started our new role as part of 5 Brigade. This was a very busy commitment as far as peacetime roles go, our job was to be ready for deployment on a worldwide scale. This meant lots of long training exercises, not forgetting the obligatory six month deployment to Northern Ireland, more on that later... My first few months back in the UK were more than busy, despite my promotion there was still one major career courses I still hadn't done. A course normally carried out pending imminent promotion to Sergeant. Through no fault of my own it was a course I should have done during those earlier years spent as a young sergeant, however due to my role sneaking around in Northern Ireland I never got chance to do it. As far as infantry courses goes this was the one you needed under your belt. This was the Platoon Sergeants Battle Course at Brecon in South Wales, including the first phase at the School of Infantry in Warminster. All in all twelve weeks of separation, just the thing you need to be doing during the winter months in UK (*joke*), also slightly ironic that I used the excuse of separation just a few months earlier for not going on SAS selection. The first five week phase at Warminster was quite scary at times, as this involved planning and conducting live firing exercises, what made it scarier, was the fact that you were solely responsible if something went wrong. Live firing exercises are part and parcel of infantry soldering. Over the years quite a number of soldiers have been killed during live firing exercises, give people weapons and get them to run around in the undergrowth firing at shit and something can quite easily go wrong, if it's not planned properly, or someone takes their eye of the ball. I remember being told that one of the reasons they give platoon sergeants this qualification is that should something go wrong it is far easier to hang a platoon sergeants than a higher ranking officer. The shit rolls down hill and stops at you. During my career there have been some moments when I thought this is the day, non-more so when I was the conducting officer on a grenade throwing range with members of the TA. The grenade range was without question the one we all feared as conducting officers, as you are totally reliant on the guys in the throwing bay to do their job. At the time this was my second posting to the TA as a PSI (Permanent Staff Instructor), as one of the few qualified to run the range I was appointed with this task. Although I had lots of admiration for members of the TA it was still a daunting prospect to hand what can only be described as a ticking time bomb to a group of part timers. As regular infantry soldiers on average you get to throw live grenades at least once sometimes twice a year, it is very rare for TA soldier's to be given the opportunity during peacetime training. So you can imagine their excitement when given the news that they were going to be throwing a live high explosive grenade. This excitement soon turned to sheer fear for some as they trembled in the throwing bay as they were handed the body of the grenade then the detonator, which was screwed into the body, priming the grenade before throwing. On the day over 180 members of the TA including a small number of women turned up to throw at least two grenades each, this was a once in a lifetime opportunity for most of them. It was my job to oversee the safety of the range, prior to throwing the live grenade they had all carried out the necessary training. Not forgetting the horror stories told by the so called old sweats, all telling tales of the things that can go wrong. Which went something like this:

"One lad in the next throwing bay to me pulled the pin on his grenade right, and it just went off, blew his fucking arm off. It landed in my throwing bay, honest to god. There was this other time right, when this other lad threw his grenade, it hit the top of the wall and bounced into the next throwing bay and killed the other two who were waiting to throw". I am sure you get the idea.

The standard grenade range consists of two throwing bays, priming bays, waiting areas and a control tower where I stood to orchestrate the proceedings. The control tower was the safest place to be when the throwing starts, but if the grenade failed to explode for whatever reason it was my job to walk out to the location of the unexploded grenade and quite simply blow it up. It's not the unexploded grenade that scares you it's the fact that you have to add more explosives, creating an explosive charge, then light a length of fuse and walk away praying that you have set everything up correctly. Being blown up by someone else is a hazard of the job, but blowing yourself up is just a fecking tragedy. With over 180 troops throwing grenades all day you can guarantee some won't detonate for one reason or another. Pulling a pin from a live grenade gives you a strange feeling, a mixture of power and fear, all in one; loosen your grip or drop it and you have got less than three seconds before the fecking thing explodes. As you can imagine there were some scary moments, without sounding sexist girls are not particularly renowned for their throwing technique, there were some grenades that just made it over the wall that separated and protected the thrower from the exploding grenade, fortunately no one was killed or injured. It was a long day, as I watched from the tower as the final grenade was thrown, I was about to breathe that final sigh of relief. I watched it land, and ducked down waiting for the explosion which never came. Shit… shit… shit… We now had to wait for 15 minutes or was it 30? However it was enough time to read through Pamphlet 21 the holy bible for conduct and safety on the range. This was a time in your life when things were quite literally done by the book. After the designated soak period I picked up my red box containing my explosive kit and took the long lonely walk out to the grenade to set the explosives needed to destroy the grenade, after lighting the 30 second fuse I walked back, took up my position of safety, praying for the thing to explode….BANG! Thank fuck for that. It was a big bang as I added a little bit more than the required amount of explosives just to make sure. My training at Warminster had paid off, I had survived this little episode. Once we finished phase one we travelled to South Wales and the famous Brecon Beacons to complete our Platoon Sergeants Tactics Course. Seven weeks of pain were about to follow. The problem I had was that unlike my fellow candidates on the course I was already at the rank of Staff Sergeant, and at twenty eight no doubt the oldest on the course, which some found strange, especially the instructors. In their opinion it was clear that I was only doing this course to get the tick in the box, it was merely a formality. In my opinion I was just like everyone else, I was there to learn. Unfortunately my squad instructor seemed to take an instant dislike to me and at one point actually said while holding up his pen and I quote "I can destroy you with this". There were others in the room at the time and he said he was making a general comment during his opening address to the squad. But both I knew and he knew, he was referring to me. This wasn't a moment of paranoia he really didn't like me. Remember this was a career course and he was referring to the report you get at the end of course. There were some top instructors at Brecon but on rare occasions units would send anyone to fill the slot. We obviously got the guy who was filling the slot, he actually looked out of place, he was a slightly overweight Guardsman, it wasn't just his appearance, he was a poor instructor. On one occasion he was delivering content on a tactics lesson that was out of date, reading direct from a Pamphlet, one we all had amended before we arrived, it was clear to us that he was ill prepared. We all looked at each other with that, is this guy for real kind of look. We all started to lose confidence and respect for this guy. Especially during one of the main fitness tests at Brecon, this was a two mile run in full battle kit weighing 36lbs including your helmet and rifle, which had to be completed in under 18 minutes. The last part of the course was uphill, and no matter how fit you were it still hurt. This was something the instructors would do with you, minus the helmet and the rifle, however they would carry the kit, often weighted with sand. We found out that our man had nothing in his kit, as he had unknowingly left his webbing unattended one day in the squad classroom. As one of my fellow students picked it up and declared, as he held it up with one hand he announced to us all, "he's got fuck all in his webbing, cheating bastard, he's got polystyrene in his pouches, lead by example my arse, Twat!". Physical fitness plays a big part in almost everything you do at Brecon. With less than three weeks to go I started to feel a little bit chesty, I thought I was just getting a cold or something. The runs and crawling around in the undergrowth started to get a little harder, but I continued to push myself and soldier on, big, big mistake. By the weekend of week five on this phase, I was done in. I spent that weekend in my bed hoping to recover by Monday morning when training restarted prior to the final exercise. On Sunday night I was worse than ever I started coughing up blood, all my roommates had gone home for the weekend so I was alone in the room. When Monday morning came I felt as though I was at deaths door, as some of my roommates' commented "you look fucking shit mate". It took me ages to get dressed I could hardly breathe, I thought my right lung had collapsed. Before I knew it everyone else had gone to the briefing for the final exercise. I managed to walk to the medical centre which was only a few hundred metres from the accommodation block, but it seemed to take me over an hour to reach it. As soon as I walked in I was rushed to hospital, I had contracted

Pneumonia as a result of pushing myself too far and spent the next two weeks in hospital and was subsequently RTU'd, (*returned to unit*). I was gutted this was a course I needed to complete, although it wasn't something I wanted to do all over again either. When I got home Linda had no idea what had happened and wasn't even aware that I was admitted to hospital.

Less than four weeks later I found myself back in Brecon, I had to complete the last three weeks of the course. If I didn't go back now I would've had to do the whole thing again in a few months' time. It wasn't easy going back, understandably my fitness level had dropped as I still hadn't fully recovered from my Pneumonia. I also had to join a group who had been together for the past nine weeks. Plus Linda was now almost eight months pregnant. This was not the ideal situation, but as always Linda just let me get on with it, as I uttered those immortal words, *"don't worry love I will be back before our little man is born"*, although we had no idea what sex our new baby was going to be. I was just praying that Linda would hold on for few more weeks. With less than two weeks to go Linda was admitted and went into labour on Monday afternoon on the 18th July, our Tom was on his way. Fortunately Linda's mum and dad were staying with us at the time, it was her mum who made the call to the admin office in Brecon to notify them that my wife had gone into labour. I wasn't told until we returned from training later that day. I asked my instructor if I could leave, to be there for the birth, to be honest I can't even remember if he said yes or no, I just knew if I went I would have to be back for first parade the next day. So I jumped in my car to take the 246 mile drive from Brecon to Canterbury, a drive that normally takes over four hours, I think I did it in three, I was desperate to be there, I'd promised. I thought I would have plenty of time, Linda was in labour for about thirteen hours when Mark was born, but it was not to be, Tom beat me to it and arrived about thirty minutes before me and was in her arms when I arrived. Linda was pleased to see me but it was a flying visit, I just needed to know they were both OK, less than two hours later I was on my way back to Brecon to prepare for the final exercise. I finally completed the course, however it wasn't the best report I have had in my career. I suppose the fat Guardsman was right, although he was long gone when I returned for the second time, his previous report was taken into account. I still passed the course and had my tick in the box. Senior Brecon was finally done and dusted. Although some of the comments on the report were not that favourable, apparently he had written my fitness level was quite poor, *errrrr Pneumonia dickhead*. It also stated that I gave the impression that I didn't need to or want to be there, yes its true I did have other things on my mind. *(I think my wife was pregnant at the time)*. Sorry that's my attempt at sarcasm. To be honest very few of us really wanted to be there, although Brecon and South Wales is without doubt a beautiful part of the country, there is only so much enjoyment you can get from running around the Brecon Beacons, both in winter and at the height of summer in July. So yes at times none of us wanted to be there, and yes I was glad that this chapter in my life was over, but returned to Brecon and the Sennybridge training area many more times in my career and loved it.

The Best Loser

Top: Y Company Boxing Team 1981 Champion Company Me front Left **Bottom**: Battalion Boxing Team Berlin, spot the World Champion Back Row, Front Row: Jock Stacy, Me, Mac Macdonald. Back Row Nigel, Kev Doyle, Big John Benn, (Nigels Brother) George Jay, Gibbo.

239

Top Photo: On patrol in the Ardoyne Belfast 1981, during the Hunger Strikes.
Bottom Photo: At a Christmas function somewhere in Dungannon, East Tyrone, with members of Special Branch Christmas 1984, probably thinking of home.

Always ready to perform

Let's put a smile on that face of yours!

Me performing my famous chicken routine in the Sergeant mess in Ballykelly, Northern Ireland 1984. On a rare occasion when I went back to visit the Battalion.

Not quite sure what the facial expression was for at the time?

Well that's all folks. Looks like the chicken had a good night. Check out the glass near the guitar.

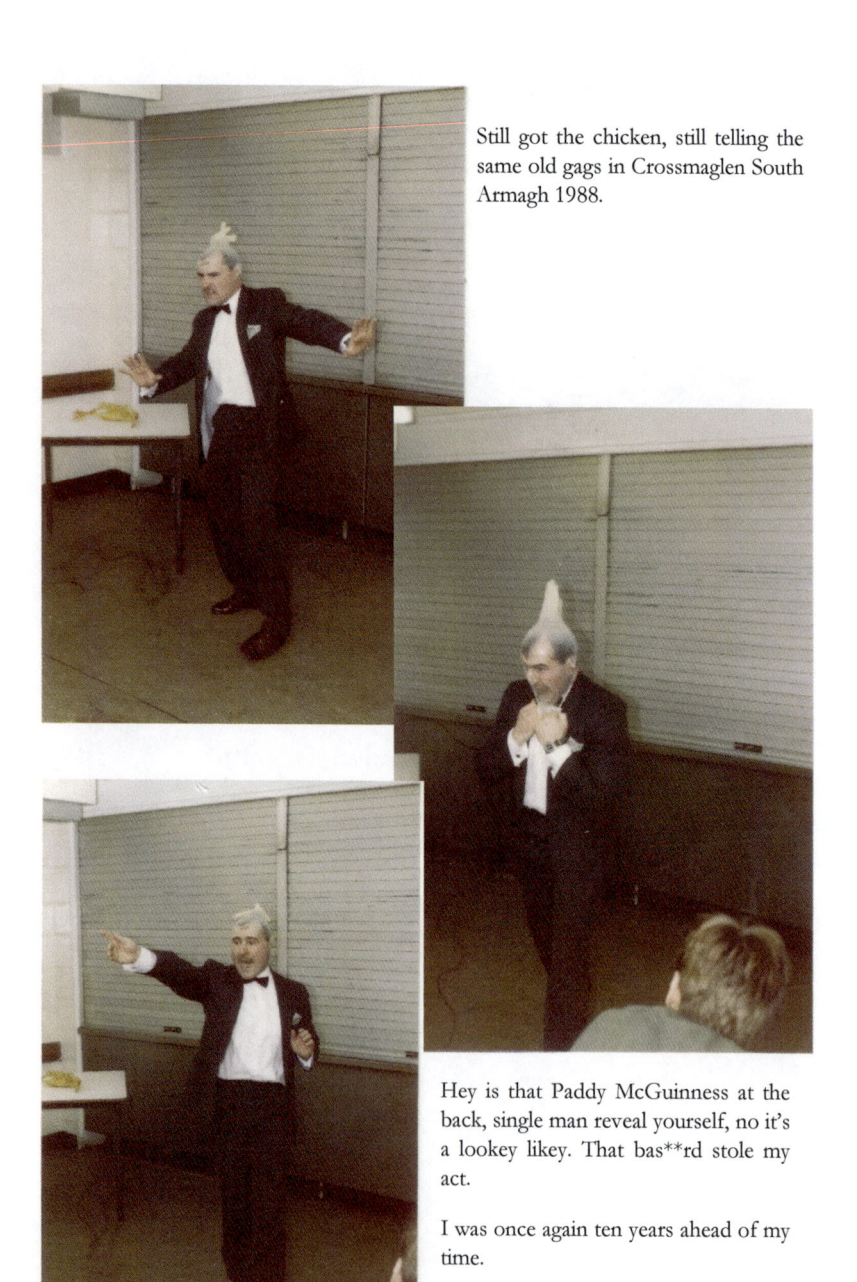

Still got the chicken, still telling the same old gags in Crossmaglen South Armagh 1988.

Hey is that Paddy McGuinness at the back, single man reveal yourself, no it's a lookey likey. That bas**rd stole my act.

I was once again ten years ahead of my time.

FAST FORWARD 23 YEARS
From Crossmaglen to the famous Comedy Store in Manchester looking confident, and at home on stage. **November 2011.**

It was great to play my old self again, but on seeing these pictures I realised I had to lose that weight.

I almost beat the GONG!

245

Left: Receiving the GOCS Commendation 1987 in Cyprus.

Right: The last picture taken of me in uniform March 2000, a month before I left the Army, obviously thinking long and hard…

Left: Presented with the British Empire Medal (BEM), Woodlands Camp, Germany 1990.

Me Pumping Iron in Crossmaglen 1989

Right: Me Showing off in the Sgt Mess Londonderry 1998, pressing a full 72kg beer keg above my head 10 times.

Me far right, posing with the Oldham posse for this picture for the Oldham Chronicle Londonderry 1998…. I think?

247

The Chuckle Brothers Run for Charity.

This is what the Brownlee Brothers will look like in 25 years' time.

Me & Paddy At the start of the Great North Run 2010 Running for Charity,

FAST at 50
Fit and Still Training at 50.

Me and Paddy at another crazy event in November 2012, with the British Military Fitness Team, I can't believe we paid to enter a competition we used to do for free. BTW it looks like a nice day but it was feckin freezing.

Above: Just before the start of the London Marathon 2010

Below: Me finishing the Oldham Half Marathon in less than two hours. 2012 one of the toughest in the country.

249

Chapter 32

Helicopters, Dancing Girls & Medals

With Brecon behind me it was now time to return to Canterbury and settle back into family life. Although in the army there wasn't much in the way of normality to the family life we had. When I returned from Brecon Thomas was just a few weeks old, many modern fathers of today would take some kind of paternity leave, however this was not a pre requisite as far as the army is concerned. I'm not sure if it's the same today, perhaps nothing has changed. You are without question married to the job, at the time you never question it, work life balance was not something we had even heard of. Linda was yet again left holding the baby, quite literally, as we received notification that we were being deployed to Crossmaglen in South Armagh, for another six month tour in Northern Ireland. This would mean Christmas away from the family, something we were now starting to get used to.

After the usual period of training we deployed to Crossmaglen in early November 1988. I arrived as part of the advanced party just days after a mortar attack on the base, the blast damage was still evident on the Southside of the perimeter fence, and one mortar did land in the base but fortunately failed to explode. This was quite a common occurrence in the history of the security base and RUC station in Crossmaglen. It was something we came to expect at least once during a six month tour in South Armagh. Life inside the base was quite hectic, not to mention cramped.

Helicopters Dancing Girls and Medals

Especially the living space, with bunk beds stacked three high, which were aptly nicknamed the subs (*submarine*), due to the amount of room you had, or should I say didn't have. It was made worse when we had other troops visiting from other units and Special Forces when a major operation was ongoing. At times there could be over 300 military personal living and working in this small base. It was without doubt a prime target over the years.

As the CQMS I had my work cut-out, I have used that phrase (*idiom*) a few times now and have this image of people sat around a craft table with scissors and fuzzy felt, creating a collage of my job description, it's crazy how the mind works. It's a phrase we all use and are familiar with but I have never really thought about it before, it's not until you write something down a few times you start to think WTF, and who's cutting this work out for me anyway.

So let's get back to the story… the unit we took over from had three other SNCO's sometimes four working alongside their CQMS. In addition to maintaining all the equipment at the base the CQMS was also responsible for administering all the outposts, these were the famous OP's and Sangers strategically placed along the border. These were permanently manned during the height of the troubles, and were themselves prime targets. Nothing moved by road everything was flown in, so helicopters were a big part of my daily routine. Unlike my predecessors I never had the luxury of having the three other SNCO's working alongside me, (*because I had my work cut out and somebody must have lost those pieces*). I just had the normal allocation of two junior storemen. Each day I would take one of them with me to deliver supplies and collect broken equipment or replace it from the observation posts and outstations. We had a simple system, equipment was placed in clear plastic bags and rubbish was placed in black bin liners. I lost count of how many times the troops got this wrong, as you heard the distinctive smashing sound of something expensive hitting the tarmac, when the loadmaster threw the bags from the helicopter. At the weekend we would fly into Bessbrook Mill, (*the busiest heliport in Europe, no doubt the world, during the times of the troubles*), it was here were we would collect our main supplies for the base in Crossmaglen. These were placed in a large underslung load, everything from rations to toilet paper, I was responsible for everything in the load, quite often this would amount to thousands of pounds. On one occasion the NAAFI manager at Bessbrook asked me if he could put a box on my load just before we were about to leave, he said it was for NAAFI canteen. I failed to ask him which canteen and what was in the box, little did I know that it would almost cause the aircraft to crash, with me in it. We were in the air for about 5 minutes when the loadmaster grabbed me by the collar and forced my head out of the open door to show me what was going on. We were about 300 feet off the ground at the time, flying over the emerald green countryside of South Armagh. The box the NAAFI manger put on had crushed as the top of the net tightened when the aircraft took off. The box contained hundreds of white polystyrene cups for one of the vending machines, these where now flying all over the countryside, some were almost hitting the tail rotor. He indicated to me that he was going to drop the load, by moving his hand over his neck in a chopping motion, I shook my head... NO! The quartermaster will fuckin kill me if you do that, there's over half a million pounds worth of night sights and thermal imagers down there. Although the wind was now whistling around the cockpit, I heard him say as he put his mouth right up against my ear, "if any of those fucking cups go anywhere near that air inlet I am dropping this fucker, capeesh! *("I thought, you're not even Italian")*. Fortunately for me the cups soon stopped flying out of the box. When we landed and unloaded the offending item, in my frustration I kicked it across the helipad. I could see that marked on the box in large black letters were the initials FLK, it wasn't even our fecking box, it was for Forkhill, which was about 8 miles east of Crossmaglen.

To identify your items for the designated flight you would clearly mark them in the same way civilian commercial flights mark baggage, Crossmaglen was abbreviated to XMG, the base at neighbouring Forkhill was FLK, and Bessbrook Mill was abbreviated to BBK etc.

The helicopter flights throughout Northern Ireland were coordinated to precision, even more so in South Armagh, resulting in a daily changing time table, (flight bids). There were very strict rules when it came to the loads the choppers were carrying, be it equipment or passengers (PAX). Filling out flight bids was part of my daily routine, and helicopters were now part of my everyday life. If I wasn't in one I was unloading one. Although my main place of residence was at the base in Crossmaglen, I was often left stranded at various

OP's especially at G40 if the weather closed in unexpectedly, which undoubtedly restricted flying. There were many more close calls which didn't involve polystyrene cups, the threat of attacks on helicopters was quite high, and understandably they were prime targets in South Armagh.

When I first went to the careers office to join the army all those years ago, and said that I wasn't sure what I wanted to do, but wanted to jump out of helicopters, I suppose that part of my career was well and truly fulfilled. I fully enjoyed my time in South Armagh, and although very busy and away from my family, the time seemed to pass very quickly, no doubt as a result of the constant workload. There was very little time for recreation, although I still found time to do a spot of weight training, and apart from the four days R&R, time off was a rarity. However on occasion during operational tours there would be some form of entertainment. These would be organised by an organisation known as Combined Services Entertainment, (CSE Show). Quite often these CSE shows would include some main stream entertainers, manly comedians, like Jim Davidson, Bobby Davro, Bradley Walsh, to name but a few. There would also be dancers to add a little glamour (*eye candy*), to the entertainment. The aim of these shows were to help break up the routine, and in some way assist in boosting moral. It was very rare for any of these entertainers to travel to Crossmaglen, nevertheless this did not stop my company commander putting in a request. At the time there was a small show doing the so called circuit, it included a four piece troop of exotic dancers, the type that kept their clothes on, a bit like the famous Hot Gossip dancers of the early eighties. During one of the daily meetings the company commander, who was fondly known as "Ming the Merciless" due to his stop at nothing kind of attitude. Set me the task of getting this troop of entertainers to perform in Crossmaglen, not the easiest request to fulfil. However I managed it, the flight was booked for 8 PAX which included the four lovely ladies, two singers a comedian plus the tour manager. Over 100 troops were assembled in the small cookhouse all eager to see these lovely ladies, everything was organised, until they arrived at Bessbrook to take the helicopter flight to Crossmaglen. At the last minute the tour manager added another two entertainers to his troop, when they went to board the chopper they were turned away as there were now too many of them. Resulting in none of them actually getting on the flight. Remember these flights were strictly coordinated there was no time to wait around while they decided who was and who wasn't getting on. Ming was none too happy when he found out that they had all been turned away, in fact at one point I saw him punching walls, not something you would expect from a future Brigadier. He gave me that look, and without saying a word I knew it was down to me to save the day. There were over 100 troops waiting to be entertained. Fortunately I had packed my black suit and bow tie, and once again I found myself performing my routine in the canteen, in front of a mob who were expecting scantily clad dancing girls. I don't know how I managed it but I survived, as I improvised and added some new gags to my routine. I was once again enjoying the attention, I'd never felt so comfortable and confident, it was a great feeling as the laughter echoed around the canteen.

My efforts in Crossmaglen earned me the British Empire Medal (BEM), although at the time as far as I was concerned I was just doing my job. I'm not referring to the comedy, but the other work I was doing, although someone in the TA, did ask me what a BEM was. So I told him I was the "Battalion Entertainments Manager". For the record I believe that my actions in Aughnacloy a few years earlier also had something to do with it. Modesty prevents me from revealing the true citation. All I can say is that in Crossmaglen I was doing the job of three men, plus sneaking around in Ireland during the mid-eighties did help.

I had no idea that I had been put forward for this award it was a complete surprise to me. Even when the letters of congratulations started to arrive from high ranking offices, which was prior to the official announcements during the Queen's Birthday Honours List. I thought... well at least Linda will get to buy a new hat and meet the Queen, sadly this wasn't to be. We never got to go to the palace, my medal was presented to me some months later in Woodlands Camp in Germany, while serving as a PSI with the Territorial Army on their annual camp. It was good to be awarded the medal in front of such a large crowd, but it would have been much nicer if my family where there and we were standing on the lawn at Buckingham Palace eating cucumber sandwiches with the Queen. (*Are well, hey-ho, that's what comes of being a Best Loser I suppose*).

Chapter 33

Married Life V The Promotion Ladder

After a successful tour in Crossmaglen we all returned home safely. Returning home from any operational deployment is a great feeling. Although separation from your family is something you come to accept as a member of the armed forces, as it simply goes with the job, but I must say it never gets any easier. Coming home to a family gives you a real sense of belonging. There is no better feeling than having someone wrap their arms around you when you finally walk through the door, especially after a long period away, plus you've got someone to give your washing to (*joking*). I suppose that's one of the reasons many soldiers marry quite young, we all want someone to come home to. I remember the times when I have returned from a period away to my empty barrack room/bunk, and once you have unpacked your kit, you are just left with a pile of dirty washing and a Pot Noodle.

Life as a soldier can be quite lonely sometimes despite that fact you are not completely alone, if you know what I mean. As you rise up the ranks the accommodation does improve, including all the creature comforts. But nothing beats walking through camp to your married quarter, to find your wife and family waiting for you with open arms. Although there were times when the atmosphere can be a little different. In the words of a famous actor and wordsmith, *"life isn't all sunshine and rainbows"*.

Not long after the tour in South Armagh we spent six weeks in Kenya, which I mentioned earlier. In fact is was eight weeks for me as I once again deployed with the advance party on Boxing Day 1989. Not the best time to leave, especially when most of your friends and neighbours are still enjoying a rare Christmas break together, and looking forward to the New Year. Linda was none too happy when I told her that I was leaving for Kenya, there is a difference with going away on operations and going away on exercise, especially when it's to somewhere with a much warmer climate thousands of miles away. Although there is very little you can do about it at the time, our conversations were often very one sided. *"Why do you have to go, he's not going next-door until the second week in January… It's my job love I have to go, were did you put the suntan lotion?"* These are words I would find myself saying many times during my long career. It was quite true, it was my job, (*I was joking about the suntan lotion*). I was after all climbing the promotion ladder. I suppose I could have kicked up a fuss and come up with an excuse for not leaving early, but there was very little chance of that. You know when you are not in the good books when the letters from home aren't as frequent. They say that absence makes the heart grow fonder, that all depends on the circumstances, not everyone makes it as a married couple in the army. The wives have to put up with so much, which like many I took for granted, I was without doubt career driven. As far as I was concerned I was doing it for the family, my view was that the higher you climb the better the prospects. After so much separation we decided that living in married quarters was not the best, especially as the

Married Life V The Promotion Ladder

commitments and demands on the armed forces increased, I was constantly away. Plus every two years we were uprooting the family and moving somewhere different. This no doubt had an effect on the kids, especially Mark as he was bounced from one school to another.

Fortunately after Canterbury I was posted to the Territorial Army as Permanent Staff Instructor (QPSI), at the time this was in fact considered a career posting. I would be serving with one of our sister Battalions 5 RRF, at C Company, based in Ashton under Lyne. This was the perfect posting for me as it meant that both Linda and I were much closer to our families. It couldn't have come at a better time. As Mark was also about to start secondary school, so we decided it was time to call it quits on married quarters. We needed somewhere more permanent, so we set about the task of buying our own home. It didn't take us long to find the perfect property, and by October 1990 we were living in our own home. Life was perfect for a while, it was like living in a 9 till 5 kind of world, with the odd weekend away. Life with the TA was very good and that two years seemed to fly by. Sadly this was also the time when our Mick suffered a massive brain haemorrhage. Serving close to family meant that I was there to offer my full support. If I was serving anywhere else this would not have been possible, fate I suppose. This time I was without doubt in the right place at the right time. However these things never last and before I knew it I was heading back to the battalion, on promotion to WO2 (Company Sergeant Major), but there was a twist in the tail.

Before going back to the battalion I was called to a meeting, prior to which, we were notified of the proposed cuts to our regiment, basically our three regular battalions were to be cut to two. This would take effect during the summer of 1992. What this meant was that there where now less appointments to fill in the future, making promotion even more competitive. The First and Third Battalions were to become one, and after the merger there was going to be a surplus of manpower, basically a company strength of over 120 troops including officers and SNCO's. I was told that this group of people most of which had volunteered, would be posted out of the Battalion to join the Irish Guards for their first ever tour of Northern Ireland. We would remain Fusiliers but on paper we would be part of the Irish Guards establishment/contingent in Northern Ireland serving in Fermanagh. I was told that I was selected to be the CSM of this company, *(apparently something to do with my previous experience)*, and to be ready to join them in Perbright, in preparation for the start of their Northern Ireland training, before being deployed to Fermanagh in November that year. (*"Shit not another Christmas in Northern Ireland beckoned"*). Before this I was to return to the First Battalion who were at the time in Tidworth and the company I was joining were about to deploy to Jamaica for a six week exercise. This I suppose was my sweetener, to soften the blow of yet another operational tour of Northern Ireland. What could I say, it's not as if I was in a position to say no. Unfortunately it wasn't the way Linda saw it. I was once again putting my career first. When I returned home to give Linda the news, she was pleased I was being promoted, she was a little disappointed that I would be yet again spending another Christmas in Northern Ireland, and yes you guessed it, when I asked her were the suntan lotion was because I was jetting off to Jamaica in a couple of weeks she was not happy, it's fair to say she was flipping upset somewhat, (*toned it down there, she was in fact fucking furious*).

Chapter 34

Living Separate Lives

I joined the Irish Guards as they were about to embark on their Northern Ireland training. This would be their first tour so everything was new and exciting. Although the odd individual had previously served in Northern Ireland on attachment, this was the very first time the Regiment as a whole had served here, there was lots for them to learn. As part of my role I too had something new to learn and attended the Search Advisors Course, at the Royal Engineers Depot in Chatham. Searching for arms and explosives was both exciting and without doubt dangerous. This two week course taught us all the skills you needed to plan and conduct searches in both rural and urban environments', plus we got the chance to play with some new and exciting pieces of kit. It also gave me an opportunity to meet some of the other WO2s from the Irish Guards before I officially took up permanent residence with them in Perbright. The course also gave me an opportunity to get to know some of my own search team commanders before we all formed our new company.

This was a rare opportunity, the chance to form a brand new company, (*B Company*) it wasn't something that happens that often and I was at the centre of it all. Some may say a good career move, as this would mean that the annual report I would receive at the end of this attachment would come from a totally independent source, outside of my own regiment and division, my chance to shine once again. All in all we had a very successful tour with the Irish Guards although it wasn't completely trouble free, in fact we had three major incidents in one week. Like buses you can wait for ages before you see one, then three come your way in quick succession. During the early 90,s there was a significant threat of sniper attacks within the border regions of South Armagh and Fermanagh. Northern Ireland was still quite active right up until, the mid-nineties, prior to the Good Friday Agreement.

This time in my life was also the start of another long period away from my family, our separate lives had begun. When we returned from Ireland we remained with the Irish Guards for a few weeks until we all re-joined our own battalion in Warminster. However this was not before attending the Irish Guards Summer Ball. Over the years I have been to many large functions and this was by far a grand affair. Linda came down for the weekend and we had a great time. People often ask me if I miss my time in the army and I always reply with the same answer. I would say that the one thing most ex-servicemen and women miss is without doubt the social scene, be it a large summer ball or simply a get together at a happy hour in the mess.

On returning to my own unit sadly B Company was absorbed into the existing structure of the Battalion, which was a shame as we had formed quite an effective team and had achieved a great working relationship over the past twelve months. In my next job I took up the post as CSM (*Company Sergeant Major*) Y Company, our role in Warminster was perhaps one of the busiest peacetime roles a unit could get. Our primary job was to support all the major exercises at the School of Infantry, basically we provided all the manpower and administrative support for everything that went on there, (*a role fondly known as the Demo Battalion*). Salisbury Plain was a second home to us, at times it was very demanding and time off was a rarity. When I did get a weekend off I would commute the long drive home, in total a 390 mile round trip, a journey which on a Friday night could take you anything from four to eight hours depending on the state of play at the notorious M5 and M6 Spaghetti Junction, no sooner had I got home, it was time to turn around and go back.

I remember someone once saying *"you must love your wife if you do that every weekend"*. I must admit at times it was hard especially after a busy week. I remember there were times when I would drive down the motorway with my head out of the window, just to keep myself awake. Quite often singing at the top of my voice the words to the song by 10CC *"The things we do for love"*.

"All together now…. Like driving through the rain and the snow when there's nowhere to go and you think part of you is dying if these cars don't get out of my way I'll be cryin.

I think I'm going to breakdown….. Fuck! Ti Fuck! Ti Fuck!

Ooo the things we do for love, the things we do f luv eh."

What do you expect I'm Northern…? It was all worth it though, especially when I had a pile of washing (*joke*). Living and commuting from Warminster soon became routine, as more married SNCO'S started living in.

It became the new trend partly due to the commitments brought on by the ever increasing demand on the armed forces. With many of us now choosing to buy our own homes and get on the property ladder. When we did get time off it was best spent in your own home, plus when the time came for re-deployment you didn't have all the upheaval of finding new schools for the kids. We found that no sooner had we unpacked our MFO Boxes it was time to re-pack them and move again. (*Although we did miss the disturbance allowance*).

After less than 18 months in Warminster I was on the move again, this time I was posted to Coventry for another stint with the TA, this time as the Senior Permanent Staff Instructor (SPSI), with HQ Company 5RRF. This move meant that I was now much closer to home, but not quite close enough to allow me the flexibility to make a daily commute. I spent most weekdays living in digs, a bed and breakfast in the centre of Coventry. Working with the TA meant that most weekends where spent on a training area somewhere, this could be anywhere from Dartmoor in the southwest of the country to Warcop or Otterburn in the north and northeast. When training was over we would travel all the way back to Coventry on Sunday morning, and when I could I would then jump in my car and drive home. Only to return on Monday morning to be back at work before 10.00am. This was not by any means perfect, and after a while it no doubt takes its toll on the relationship. We were now without doubt leading very separate lives. Somehow we managed to keep it together and before long we had another baby on the way.

Louis arrived on the 23rd of October 1995, he arrived a few days early, but this time I was there for the birth. We now had three sons all born just over seven years apart, no doubt a sign that I had spent far too much time away. God knows how many kids we would have had if I had been home more often. One thing was evident and something I still regret today, I missed so much of them growing up, especially Mark and Tom. This is something I still beat myself up about as I am not sure what influence I have had on them, perhaps one day they will tell me. I remember one occasion when Tom was about 5 or 6 years old, he was asked to draw a picture of his family, and you guessed it, I wasn't in it. When Linda asked him, why is dad not in the picture? He said dad doesn't live in our house, it's strange how a child's mind works but he was right. Although at the time I didn't give it much thought, I just got on with what I thought my role in life was, which in my opinion, was to simply do my best to support my family financially, I was after all the bread winner. Everything I was doing was for them... wasn't it?

Today I know it's a different story, there are without doubt some things I would go back and change, I am sure I could have done so much more. I never realised at the time that Linda was fighting post-natal depression, during those first few months after giving birth to Louis. I most certainly wasn't very supportive, in the words of my wife "I was a shit", she was without doubt right. I had other priorities in my life. I really jeopardised our relationship during this period in our lives. We came very close to splitting up.

Chapter 35

The Final Push to Success

After successfully completing my posting with the TA, it was time to re-join my battalion. They had not long returned from a tour in Bosnia and where now on their way for yet another two year tour in… drum roll please… yes, you guessed it, Northern Ireland. This time I was posted to Londonderry, were I was promoted to RQMS (T) (*Regimental Quartermaster Sergeant*) and at 36 this meant I was now only one short step from reaching my goal. I was also reunited with my old mentor, the one and only, and now Major Mick Moran QGM, AKA "*Metal Micky*" who now had even more medals. He was now the Quartermaster, master of all he surveyed. He was without doubt the gaffer, his opposite number was Captain Bob, he was my immediate boss and was one step ahead of Micky in the meals race, in that he was the recipient of the MBE, a medal Micky no doubt had his sights set on. Along with my good friend Dave Wink, who was the other RQMS, we formed the head shed of the Quartermasters' Department. In fact we were quite unique, as we were all from Oldham, ironically the RSM, big Jimmy was also from Oldham. Together we were fondly known as the Oldham Posse, as it was very rare that five lads from a small town like Oldham, would hold such key positions in a Regiment, especially at the same time. Our picture actually appeared in the Oldham Chronicle, it was fame for the famous five, it could be said that together we actually ran the Battalion.

This particular tour was unlike any other I had been on previously. Northern Ireland was a much quieter place after the Good Friday agreement, plus my role was much more of an administrative one, not that I was complaining, at times it was full on 24/7 kinda stuff. Like any large organisation there is a lot going on behind the scenes and the Quartermasters' department is a busy place to be, especially on an operational tour.

During my time in Londonderry Linda remained on the mainland. We could have moved back into married quarters but chose not to, as it would mean disrupting the kids, especially Mark as he was now approaching his final years in school, plus Linda wasn't too keen on the idea. I managed to get home for a long weekend at least once every six weeks or so. It actually took me less time to get home from Northern Ireland than it did from Coventry, I could be home in under Two hours on a good day. During my second year in Londonderry I started to concentrate on what I was going do with my future, although leaving the army still seemed a million miles away, as up until this point I was in it for the long hall. A few of us decided that we should study for a degree during our spare time. I'm not quite sure how this came about, but it may have had something to do with having more access to computers. Plus a number of us where already studying for a Level 5 NVQ Diploma in Management and Leadership. (*See we're not all thick in the Infantry*). While searching for a course to add a little more substance to my knowledge of the commercial world, I stumbled on the subject of Marketing and subsequently enrolled on a correspondence course. Within a few days I was hooked as I found the fundamentals of the marketing process to be based on what I thought was just common-sense. This was the subject for me, exploring the philosophy of "why do we buy, what we buy" intrigued me and still does. Sometimes we buy things purely on impulse, one of my impulse purchases was a £450.00 Saxophone, which I bought in Coventry while serving with the TA. Prior to buying my own I did have one on loan from the band. This was a large battered old Tenor Saxophone, which I used mainly as a prop while performing my comedy routine. I would do a whole routine with it hanging from neck never actually playing it, I just blew a few notes now and again and carried on with gags. I can't remember all the gags, but I remember walking on once and saying, *"I've just joined the Jazz Club... I thought it would be cool, but it's full of WANKERS! ... No sorry that's the Jizz Club"*. Agggggggh that was awful, and people ask me why I never made it as a comedian. I did eventually learn to play the saxophone... so when I wasn't studying for my degree I would annoy everyone in the mess by blowing on my saxophone. Life in the mess in Londonderry back then was great, some weekends we would start a Happy Hour on Friday afternoon and it would finish sometime on Sunday. It wasn't all just drinking and falling over, we had quite a few talented people in the mess at the time and created our own entertainment. I was also at the time the senior mess member living in the mess, so I held a position of command control, in the absence of the RSM. One impromptu event I orchestrated was on the anniversary of Elvis's death, I had told one of the young sergeants to make some stick on sideburns, which would be presented to people as they entered the mess that evening. He did not fail me in this task, as he promptly made his way to the barbershop on camp and armed with a roll of wide double-sided sticky tape he set about his task. Like a crazy Blue Peter presenter, within a few hours he had made over a 100 sets of hairy sideburns which he presented to me on a silver platter, quoting, "here's some I made earlier sir". By the end of the night everyone in the mess was wearing these things, some people even stuck them on their chest, it was just a crazy night of Elvis mayhem.

It wasn't all play and no work, both Dave and I did actually work hard during this period, and as we approached the end of the tour we were both told that we had been successful on the promotion board. And subsequently promoted to WO1.

I'd done it… from the age of 19 when I first completed the JNCOS Cadre, where we were told by the RSM at the time, that one of you sitting here today will become the RSM of this Battalion, from that day in the back of my mind I always knew he was referring to me. The problem we now faced was there where less battalions for us to be the RSM of, due to the previous restructuring of the Regiment. So who would get to be the RSM of the 1st Battalion? Traditionally it normally went to one of the RQMS's, so who was it to be, me or Dave. Well it was to be neither of us, as we both ended up being posted to the OTC (Officer Training Corps), Dave was posted to Birmingham I was posted to Newcastle. It was our old mukka from Z Company and my former sparring partner from the boxing team, Jock Stacy, who got the prize. I suppose once again I was the "Best Loser".

Chapter 36

Time to Hang up My Boots

Despite my initial disappointment of not being selected for the post as RSM of the Battalion, I was still very pleased to be promoted to WO1. When I returned from Londonderry I discussed with Linda that the post in Newcastle was one where we should be together, as it was also expected that the RSM should be accompanied by his wife on this posting. It took us a couple months to sort it out, as we had to find someone to rent our house before we moved back into a married quarter, plus wait for half term so the kids could at least start a new school during a natural break. Before we organised the family move I was staying in the Warrant Officers & Sergeants Mess at Catterick Garrison, and made the daily commute to Newcastle, while I got to grips with the job in hand. Life in the OTC as the RSM is not that dissimilar to serving with the TA, although the troops are a little different, to be honest, very different. All the officer cadets are students and undergraduates from the Neighbouring Universities of Newcastle. Some of which were destined for a career as Army Officers, while others simply thought it was a jolly good wheeze and something to do at the weekend, (*plus they got paid for doing it*). Seriously though it was quite an experience working with some of these young men and women, as many had come from very privileged backgrounds. These young people believe it or not would become the movers and shakers of commerce and industry in the future. So who knows what influence this crazy little fellow from Oldham may have had on some of them, all good I hope?

My primary job as the RSM was to help plan and organise most of the training. Together with a small team of permanent staff instructors (PSIs), working alongside me, we would organise the weekends training and major exercises. This could be anything from conducting live firing exercises to a full blown two week survival exercise in Scotland.

When Linda and the kids finally joined me we moved into a large new four bedroomed detached house on the outskirts of Newcastle close to the A1. We had managed to rent our house, so we just broke even when it came to paying the mortgage and rent for the house we were now living in. Mark had now left school and soon found a job working at the local Sainsbury's supermarket. Tom was ten and about to start secondary school, Louis who was now almost four and started at the local nursery close to where we lived. Family life was quite normal again, the months soon passed and it wasn't long before it was time for me to consider hanging up my boots.

As you will have read in the earlier chapters you will know what happened next, however I only skimmed over how I was feeling at the time. As I approach the final chapters of the book I now feel I need to add that leaving the army no doubt contributed heavily to my bouts of depression. Many people leaving the army today talk about post-traumatic stress, often relating it to things they have witnessed during their time as serving soldiers, believing that it is these images that trigger the anxiety. I believe that many soldiers regardless whether they have been involved in active service or not, will at some time shortly after leaving, or even in later years, especially having completed a full career, will suffer from some form of depression. At first I thought that my depression was brought on by money worries and the stress of running a failing business. Today I now believe my depression started long before that, I just didn't know it at the time. It's possible that my depression started the day I handed my kit in and signed off my 1157 (Kit Issue). Once you do that you know you are at the point of no return. Although technically you are on what is known as the reserve list, which means, if there is a major conflict you could be called up again before you reach the age of 45. (*For the record I believe this has now changed to 55 for those who joined the army after the 1st Apr 97*). So once you've handed your kit in basically you are OUT! ... On your own mate, which reminds me of my first experience of what leaving can do to you.

While at Newcastle as part of my resettlement I was involved with a scheme known as the "Prospects Program". In outline this was a one off program open to service leavers and ex-military personnel who were currently seeking employment in the Northeast. Some of the guys who enrolled on the course had actually been out of the army for a number of years. It ran for three consecutive months and involved a work placement with a relevant position at a local business in and around the Newcastle area. As all my current studies where based on marketing, I managed to secure a placement was with Newcastle Universities Careers Service.

This is where I became part of the steering committee and marketing team for a new web based project the University where conducting at the time. (*This is where my website knowledge began*). In addition to our time on the work placement we all attended various lectures and lessons, covering a range of business related subjects. During one of the sessions I remember we had to draw a number of pictures, illustrating where we are now, and were we would like to be in five years' time, it was something to do with goal setting and problem solving. One guy who had been a former WO2, and had been out of the army for over five years, simply drew a stickman in the centre of his page and sat there with his head in his hands looking down at the page in front of him. When asked to explain or elaborate on his illustration, he simply said, *"that's me mate I'm on my fucking own aren't I, once you leave the army you are on your fucking own pal."* I remember we all just looked at this guy and thought what the fuck… pull yourself together man you used to be a sergeant major for fuck sake. Little did I know that I was looking at a man suffering from depression, nor did I ever think that I would experience that same feeling of being on my own, despite being surround by family and friends. My first experience of this was when I went to sign on. When you first leave the army you have to go to your local Job Centre and sign on. I remember standing in the queue wearing a shirt and tie and looking around and thinking what the fuck am I doing in here. I was just another face in the crowd, a nobody looking for work. Just a few weeks ago people would stand up when I walked into a room, call me sir and respect the position I held. Now I was just the man in the queue. I now knew what he meant when he said *"I'm on my own mate"*. All that you were before counts for nothing, the world and his wife don't give a shit. This was perhaps the start of the depression, the realisation that you have spent the past 23 years in a bubble, protected by those around you and the environment in which you live.

Two days letter I registered myself as Self Employed and vowed that I would never stand in that queue again. Looking back now, I know that the depression never actually went away, it remained just below the surface, my hectic lifestyle at the time masking the symptoms. Until that day when my body, heart and soul, said that's enough! When my emotions simply exploded as I almost crumbled on the floor of the doctors' surgery.

Chapter 37

So What Now?

So what have I learned by putting all this down on paper? And where do I go from here, although I feel I have beaten my depression, there are still times when I feel down, don't we all, life is hard after all. One of the questions I wanted to find the answer to was, who am I? I don't think any of us can answer that question, I suppose it's better phrased as, who do <u>you think</u>, you are, as this is something people will often say to us, especially during a time of conflict. Our perception of who we think we are can without doubt be very different to what people actually think. So why do we care so much about what others may think. I know that I have done and achieved far more in my life than most people I know. I suppose over 100,000 words in this book is perhaps testament to that. Nonetheless when I am standing at someone's door with a parcel in my hand, I am quite simply just the man who delivers the mail, just another employee of a large company. That's what the outside world sees, as l am reminded when someone shouts from inside the house, *"who's that at the fucking door now! It's just the postman dad"*. What they don't see is what's beyond the smiling face of this humble little postman.

As I approach the end of my 55th year, I know time is ticking fast and there is still so much more I want to do with my life. There is also so much more I need to do for my family. The things you can't do when you are feeling sorry for yourself. You simply can't give if you don't feel like giving. I now know that it's TIME... that's what I need to give... **MY TIME**, something I have been far too selfish with, especially were my own family is concerned. During the course of writing this book I very rarely mentioned much about my family life, this book has all been about me. When I gave the draft of this book to my wife, one thing she pointed out to me was that there is very little in this book about them. I reminded her that they were not the problem I needed to solve, the problem was me! So who do I think I am? I am a man lucky enough to have found the key to my future happiness. I left the army in search of wealth and success, unfortunately I made the mistake of putting a monetary value on it.

So who am I? I'm the man who found the time to explore his own feelings, write them down and make them much more tangible. Looking at these words as they appear on the screen, they are still just words, they don't mean anything until someone reads them. We are all familiar with the phrase *"actions speak louder than words"* the fact that you are reading this right now shows that I finally took action. You may be reading this book simply because I asked you to or you found the cover and title intriguing, who knows you may have even paid for it. (*Thank you by the way*). Whatever the reason I hope in some way it has helped you, it may have even inspired you to write your own book. I never read many books when I was a kid, or as a young adult to be precise. I don't think I could sit still long enough. It wasn't until much later in life when I actually started reading books, these were mainly self-help books. The first book I read from cover to cover without actually putting is down was

So What Now?

"*Think and Grow Rich by Napoleon Hill*". Once I read it, I then went on to read it many more times. I found myself re-reading whole chapters over and over, mainly because at the time I wanted to find the secret to wealth. I believed the answers where somewhere hidden in the words of that book. If you have read it you may know what I mean, every time you re-read a chapter you will find different meaning or perspective to what is written. Now I have written my own book it all starts to make more sense to me, perhaps that was the answer, I needed to write my own book. What does it actually mean, to think and grow rich? It wasn't until I continued to read the chapter on auto suggestion that I finally started to work it out. If you read this poem from the book you may start to see exactly what I mean.

"If you think you are beaten, you are,
If you think you dare not, you don't
If you like to win, but you think you can't,
It is almost certain you won't.

"If you think you'll lose, you're lost
For out of the world we find,
Success begins with a fellow's will--
It's all in the state of mind.

"If you think you are outclassed, you are,
You've got to think high to rise,
You've got to be sure of yourself before
You can ever win a prize.

"Life's battles don't always go
To the stronger or faster man,
But soon or late the man who wins
Is the man **WHO THINKS HE CAN***!"*

I was always the best loser that was my problem. I always put up a good fight but never allowed myself to win. During my darker periods I read many books looking for answers, quite often I thought I found them but never really took any action. I simply let that self-doubt creep back and I was back to square one, back to being the best loser.

So what now? Now I have explored my past and above all my inner feelings I no longer see myself as a loser, my confidence is once again restored. So who knows where this book will lead me, it may even help to open a few doors, if not it will stop that table from wobbling in the kitchen, and if there are times when I do slip back to feelings of self-doubt, my wife now has something to bash me over the head with. On a more serious note writing has helped cure my own depression, it has actually taken me over three years to reach this point in the book, a great achievement for a serial procrastinator. Who knows what the future holds for me now?

Chapter 38

Back To The Future

So what does the future hold for this former soldier and humble little postman from Oldham? What I do know is that as a direct result of writing this book I now have a better understanding of the causes of my own depression. Therefore it's possible this book may go some way to helping others. For me it will be my constant reminder that I don't want to go back to that dark place. During the pre-publishing phase of writing this book I needed to find the relevant category in which to list my book, these are known as the BISAC Subject Headings. (*Book Industry Standards and Communications*) Although my book is primarily based on my autobiography and could be listed under that category. I felt that it best suited the self-help category, listing it under, SEL01100 Self-Help/Mood Disorders/Depression, basically to remind me why I wrote it in the first place. It's also without doubt a much more interesting category, plus it gives me the opportunity to expand a little more on the subject before I finally close this chapter in my life.

Understandably there is so much already written on the subject of depression and anxiety, so what makes me the expert... I'm not... I'm just someone who dealt with his own experience of it, for the record something I'm still dealing with. Mine wasn't as severe as some I'm sure, but none the less it did come to a point where I was constantly contemplating taking my own life, something I feel ashamed of. Despite everything I had achieved in my life, I felt a failure, I'd lost my self-esteem felt trapped with no way out, and therefore without doubt I was a victim of clinical depression. Something many men feel ashamed to admit. Fortunately for me I took the first step… in admitting it, not just to myself but to my GP, for the first time opening up to another human being. Once I had done that I was on a slow road to recovery.

My biggest problem at the time was that I was trying to fix all the problems in one go, I thought that once I'd admitted I was depressed it would all simply go away. As with everything in life it requires hard work. I thought it was quite simply money that caused my problems, I also used the death of my mother as an excuse for being depressed. Who knows I may have been fighting depression since the day I stood looking down at my father's grave as a fourteen year old boy. Although I now know there is a huge difference between grief and depression. Perhaps I was depressed because I hadn't yet reached my true potential?

They say that men find it much harder to acknowledge depression, however I do believe we are getting a little better at admitting it. I think we are far less macho today than we were in the 70's and 80's. Men are far more in tune with what we term as our feminine side these days. I blame Gazza for starting all that. Seriously though there is so much more in the media these days regarding depression in men, most of which seems to focus on celebrities or sportsmen. I remember seeing a program titled "The Hidden Side of Sport" hosted by Freddie Flintoff. It highlighted the common occurrence of depression in Sport, focusing on cricketers, who like many sportsman feel under pressure to achieve and remain at the top of their game despite what is happening around them. When they do underperform the media have a field day, (*pardon the pun*) which no doubt takes its toll. Sportsmen and women like service personnel also spend long periods separated from family and friends, they also follow a regime, and when this cycle ends they find it hard to adjust to the outside world of celebrity. For service personnel this would be the same as entering Civvy Street at the end of a successful career.

Creating this awareness through programmes like this has now lead to all county cricketers being encouraged to complete a series of online tutorials in a move aimed at raising awareness of depression.

No one told me during my phase of resettlement that within four of five years' time I would be contemplating taking my own life. However I have since read that the Ministry of Defence (MOD) has introduced a range of anti-stigma campaigns to encourage serving personnel to come forward to access the wide range of support that is now available. In March 2015 the MOD also joined forces with SilverCloud Health, a global provider of behavioural and mental wellness online solutions, to launch a new pilot for an online psychological wellness resource centre. Which sounds very much like the BIG WHITE WALL, a similar online platform that has been up and running for a number of years now.

Big White Wall is available free in many areas of the UK via the NHS. It is also free to all UK serving personnel, veterans, and their families. Since the war in Iraq and Afghanistan there has no doubt been an increase and more interest in the wellbeing of soldiers. The topic of post-traumatic stress disorder (PTSD), is the first thing the media seem to jump on when mental health issues are raised. Its understandable this will no doubt play a part and it's an easy label to stick on the subject of depression were ex-military are concerned. For me the underlining problem and the most common cause of depression in former servicemen is quite simply the change in regime, especially for those who enter service from a young age and complete a full career.

Many ex-servicemen will cling on to what I call the life rafts of the armed forces. They will join their local Regimental Association, some seek employment within the establishment itself. Basically keeping their hand in, they never seem to break the umbilical cord or leave the protection of the womb. Perhaps this was part of my big mistake, I totally divorced myself from the army. I only ever went to one or two Regimental reunions, when I did one of the first topics of conversion was, "you'll never guess who's dead". It was always some poor sod in his early to mid-fifties. I often wondered when it would be my turn to be the topic of conversation. Fortunately I feel I have now past that point in my life, as I look forward to the future and hope there are many more years left in me yet. Although my main concern today is my family, I would like to give something back, if by writing this book has shown that I have something to offer, if only my personal experience. I would welcome the opportunity to speak to service leavers, especially Warrant Officer and SNCO's who like me when I left the army think we are invincible. I firmly believe that if I had more of an awareness of depression prior to leaving then I would have most certainly recognized the symptoms and perhaps seeked help much sooner. Quite often I thought that asking for help showed a sign of weakness, I was of the opinion that if I didn't know the answer to something I would find it out myself, if I needed to learn a new skill I would teach myself how to do it. If I got myself in a hole I would dig myself out, thank you very much. I didn't need anyone else's help, this was my mantra.

At one of my lowest points I was sitting looking at five years of uncompleted Self-Assessment Tax Returns. During that five year period I had not submitted a tax return, I simply paid the fines for not filling them in. It was a problem I created and one I would sort out, when the sixth one arrived the problem was getting far more serious, as I was now facing potential criminal prosecution. I was in deep shit. Understandably I was fighting depression at the time, but this is not an excuse that makes the problem go away. Eventually I picked up the phone and called a help line, they told me about TAXAID a charity that helps to sort out tax problems HMRC can't sort out. It actually says that on the website, and guess what? They did, within 24hrs I was called to an office in Manchester and sat with this guy for a whole day and by the end of it he had helped me fix the problem. One that I had created, a self-inflicted wound that I allowed to fester, simply because I was of the opinion that I don't need anyone's help or advice (*what a tosser*).

So let's get back to the future, leaving the world of self-employment and joining Royal Mail has returned me to a regime like environment, this has without doubt helped me. In that everything you do on a day to day basis is structured, in a small but similar way to life in the armed forces. I start work each day at 06.30am work alongside my work colleagues for the first period of the day and then work independently delivering my quota of mail and parcels for that day. Most days I am home by 3.30pm, this is perfect for me and has allowed me to return to my studies and focus on life outside Royal Mail, allowing me to plan for the future. I still firmly believe that I have so much more to offer and I'm planning to return to some form of educational work. On occasion I still get requests from people asking about the courses I ran before my world started collapsing around me, due to my depression. The world of Internet Marketing continues to evolve, and I do still keep my finger on the pulse. However I often feel pulled in so many other directions. Whereas in the past my work ethic was all about making money I now feel life has so much more to offer. Don't get me wrong I still aim to make a living from what I do but it will no longer be a chore.

Chapter 39

Not Quite, The Final Chapter

I first started writing the notes for this book in June 2012 and as I said in a previous chapter, it has taken me just over 3 years to complete. Beating depression is quite often a long process, and writing this book has been great therapy. At times during the process I still doubted myself and often thought that what I had written was just rubbish. It wasn't until I created my book cover that I started to visualise it as a real book and not just words on a screen. When I first looked into the subject of writing a book and self-publishing, the advice I read was to just write, simply empty your thoughts on to the page, don't worry if it doesn't make sense at the time, just keep writing. Although I found this to be good sound advice, I believe you should also start with the cover design, especially during the early stages, as this allows you to visualise the completed book. I imagined it sitting on the shelf in bookshops, OK it may end up in the bargain section, but it would at least be evidence that I had started a project and finished it to the end.

If you are the type of person who flicks through a book to see what happens at the end, then you have missed an awful lot along the way. It seems like this has been a long journey, but one that has been worth it. I haven't included everything I've done in my life, and I hope there is so much more to come. I simply see this as the first edition and plan on returning to it in a few years' time to see what's changed.

One thing is for sure, I now feel I can now move on to become the person I always wanted to be.... ME!

I now know that being the best loser isn't a bad thing after all. When we lose something we can do one or two things, we can either give up completely, or we can move on and make the best of what we've got. So my final piece of advice and words of wisdom are, "simply be the best loser you can be, just move on and get on with living your own life". If depression starts to take hold of you, fight it with everything you have, and don't be afraid to ask for help, if you don't it will consume you.

Closing this chapter in my life, I'd like to give a final thank you to all my family for putting up with me throughout this journey, I love you all. xxxx

Epilogue

Mark Mooney went on to do all the things he wanted to do, after writing this book he caught the writers bug and went on to write a Sit Com for the BBC, titled *"Walk on the wild side"*. A one off six part series about Postmen and women working in the Northwest. He took his wife on a trip of a lifetime and finally visited all the wonderful places he experienced while in the army. Starting with a holiday in Bermuda and Jamaica, then on to Kenya where they flew over the Rift Valley in a hot air balloon.

He went back to the Comedy Store and beat the GONG! He took his three sons on a VIP trip to London's Leicester Square to watch a Film Premier, something he had promised many years ago. Sometimes the simple things mean so much.

He resurrected his website Fastat50.com (*Fit and still training at 50*), to encourage the over 50's to do something energetic and raise money for charity. In addition to this fitness website he also created Six Pack at 60, to prove that you can still look great as you approach retirement and beyond. He joined his younger brother in America and rode down Route 66 on a Harley Davidson trike, a trip they had planned since his brother decide to move there in 2014. He dusted off his old bucket list and in less than five years he had completed it and set about writing a new one. His alarm went off at 4.30am, he rushed to grab his pen to write all this down to publish in his book, before the memory of the dream faded.

Ten things I like about myself

All written before I started this book.

1. I have a good sense of humour.
2. I look great in a suit.
3. I work hard.
4. I never give up.
5. I can empathise with others.
6. I can run 10km in less than 50min.
7. I like myself, for liking myself. (*I think that makes sense*).
8. I like the feeling I get from helping others.
9. I like that I am not afraid anymore.
10. I like the fact that if I lose, **I am the Best Loser.**

A final BIG, BIG
Thank You!
None of this could not be possible without you, so the biggest thank you of all goes to my lovely wife Linda, for putting up with me all these years, lets hope there are many more to come.

And finally not forgetting you the reader, thanks for taking the time to read my book, I hope you found it useful. I love you too. Thanks Mark xx

Just a few final words from the author: *"If you want to make a change in your life don't just think positive, be positive, write it down, commit to it, publish it for the world to see, be held accountable for your own future, if you lose be the best loser".*

Mark Mooney September 2015.

www.bestloser.co.uk

Printed in Great Britain
by Amazon.co.uk, Ltd.,
Marston Gate.